SWU-600-004

UNIFORMS OF RUSSIAN ARMY IN THE ERA OF ANCIENT TZAR

FROM THE REIGN OF VAILI IV TO MICHAEL I, ALEXIS, FEODOR III DURING THE XVII TH CENTURY

From the Viskovatov's greatest work:
"Historical description of the clothing and
arms of the Russian Army"

SOLDIERSHOP PUBLISHING

AUTHOR

Aleksandr Vasilevich Viskovatov born 22 April (4 May New Style) 1804, died 27 February (11 March) 1858 in St. Petersburg, Russian military historian. He graduated from the 1st Cadet Corps and served in the artillery, the hydrographic depot of the Naval Ministry, and then in the Department of Military Educational Institutions. He mainly studied historical artifacts and the histories of military units. Viskovatov's greatest work was the Historical Description of the Clothing and Arms of the Russian Army.

PUBLISHING'S NOTE

NOTE ABOUT BOOK PRINTING BEFORE 1925

LICENSES COMMONS

ACKNOWLEDGEMENTS

A Special Thanks to NYPL and other institutions for their kindly permission to use some images of his archives, collections or books used in our book.

Title: **UNIFORMS OF RUSSIAN ARMY IN THE ERA OF ANCIENT TZAR**
from the reign of Vasili IV to Michael I, Alexis, Feodor III during the XVIII th Century
By A.V.Viskovatov. Serie edit by Luca S. Cristini. First edition by Soldiershop. June 2017
Cover & Art Design: Luca S. Cristini. Plates re-colorations by Anna Cristini.
ISBN code: 978-88-93272513
Published by Soldiershop publishing, via Padre Davide, 7 - 24050 Zanica (BG) ITALY. www.soldiershop.com

UNIFORMS OF THE RUSSIAN ARMY IN THE ERA OF ANCIENT TZAR

FROM THE REIGN OF VASILI IV TO MICHAEL I, ALEXIS, FEODOR III DURING THE XVIII TH CENTURY

Portrait of the Tzar Mikhail Fedorovich Romanov (1596–1645)

HISTORICAL DESCRIPTION OF THE CLOTHING AND ARMS
OF THE RUSSIAN ARMY - A.V. VISKOVATOV

Soldiershop is glad to presents the complete collection of the great job made by A.V. Viskovatov dedicated to the uniforms and weapons belonging from the first Zar and Russian emperors to the Russian army during the Napoleonic period, until 1860 about. The time we considered in this volume corresponds to the reigns of Catherine the Great (Catherine II) who reigned since 1762 until his murder on the 6 November 1796.

Our reprint in based on the original 19th century volumes, to be precise the volumes from 4 to 6 are dedicated to the reign of Catherine II; this part is distributed on 3 or 4 volumes.

Our new edition, the first ever published in English, both on paper and digital format, boasts a large number of color plates, many of them unpublished and re-coloured by our team of expert artists and scholars of uniformology. Each volume is based on 100 color plates or more, always accompanied by the original translated text which describes the subjets of the plates.

A unique work in its genre, a must have in any respecting collection!

Aleksandr Vasilevich Viskovatov born 22 April (4 May New Style) 1804, died 27 February (11 March) 1858 in St. Petersburg, Russian military historian. He graduated from the 1st Cadet Corps and served in the artillery, the hydrographic depot of the Naval Ministry, and then in the Department of Military Educational Institutions.

He mainly studied historical artifacts and the histories of military units. Viskovatov's greatest work was the Historical Description of the Clothing and Arms of the Russian Army (Vols. 1-30, St. Petersburg, 1841-62; 2nd ed. Vols. 1-34, St. Petersburg - Novosibirsk - Leningrad, 1899-1948). This work is based on a great quantity of archival documents and contains four thousand colored illustrations.

Viskovatov was the author of Chronicles of the Russian Army (Books 1-20, St. Petersburg, 1834-42) and Chronicles of the Russian Imperial Army (Parts 1-7, St. Petersburg, 1852). He collected valuable material on the history of the Russian navy which went into A Short Overview of Russian Naval Campaigns and General Voyages to the End of the XVII Century (St. Petersburg, 1864; 2nd edition Moscow, 1946). Together with A.I. Mikhailovskii-Danilevskii he helped prepare and create the Military Gallery in the Winter Palace.

He wrote the historical military inscriptions for the walls of the Hall of St. George in the Great Palace of the Kremlin. (From the article in the Soviet Military Encyclopedia.)

CONTENTS

*

STRELTSY
THE ANCIENT RUSSIAN GUARDSMEN

Streltsy (Russian: стрельцы, *streltsý*, literally "shooters"; sg. стрелец, *streléts*, "shooter", from *strelyat'* , "to shoot") were the units of Russian guardsmen from the ancient era of 16th to the early 18th centuries, armed with firearms and particular halberds.

They are also collectively known as *Marksman Troops* (стрелецкое войско). These standing forces reinforced the mounted nobility militia (поместное войско, *pomestnoe vojsko* or Landed Army) mobilized during wartime.

Origins and organization

The first streltsy units were created by the famous Tzar Ivan the Terrible sometime between 1545 and 1550 and armed with arquebuses. During his reign, Russia was fighting wars almost continuously, including the Livonian War in the North and wars against the Khanates in the South.

They first saw combat at the Siege of Kazan in 1552. Initially, the streltsy were recruited from among the free tradespeople and from the rural population. Subsequently, military service in this unit became lifelong and hereditary. Thus, while earlier in the 16th century they had been an elite force, their effectiveness was reduced by poor training and lack of choice in recruiting.

Streltsy were subdivided into *vyborniye* (выборные), or electives (later – of Moscow) and *gorodskiye* (городские), or municipal (in different Russian cities).

- The streltsy of Moscow guarded the Kremlin, performed general guard duty, and participated in military operations. They also carried out general police and fire-brigade functions in Moscow. Grigory Kotoshikhin, a Russian diplomat who had spied for and then defected to Sweden in the 1660s, reported that they used axes and buckets and copper pumps as well as hooks to pull down adjacent buildings so that fires would not spread, but Adam Olearius, a Westerner who travelled to Russia in the 17th century, noted that they never used water.
- The municipal streltsy performed garrison and border duty and carried out orders of the local administration.

Streltsy came under the control of the Streltsy Department (Стрелецкий приказ, or *Streletsky prikaz*); however, in times of war they came under their superiors. The municipal streltsy were also under the jurisdiction of the local *voevodes*.

The largest military administrative unit of the streltsy forces was *pribor* (прибор), that would later be renamed into *prikaz* and in 1681 – into regiment (полк, or *polk*). Commanders of the Streltsy unit (стрелецкие головы, or *streletskiye golovy*) and colonels in charge of regiments were chiefs of *prikazi*. They had to be nobles and appointed by the government.

The regiments (*polki*) were subdivided into *sotni* (сотни, or hundreds) and *desyatki* (десятки, or tens).

Russian Streltsy (17th century)

They could be mounted (стремянные, or *stremyanniye*; стремя (*stremya*) in Russian means "stirrup") and unmounted (пешие, or *peshiye*; пеший (*peshiy*) means "foot soldier").

Uniforms and equipment

Streltsy had identical uniforms, training and weapons. Uniforms consisted of red, blue or green coats with orange boots. Their primary weapon was an arquebus or musket, and they carried poleaxes or bardiches, and sabers for defense; some units used pikes. The longer weapons were also used to support the arquebus or musket while firing.

Service conditions

The Muscovite government was chronically short of cash and so did not often pay the streltsy well. While "entitled" to an estimated four rubles a year in the 1550s, they were often allowed to farm or trade in order to supplement their incomes. This reduced their combat effectiveness and often their desire to go on campaigns (since a season on campaign meant loss of income).Streltsy and their families lived in their own neighborhoods or districts settlements and received money and bread from the State Treasury. In certain locations, Streltsy were granted strips of land instead of money. The Streltsy settlement in Moscow was located near where the main campus of Moscow State University now stands.

Ancient Russian Militia

Military tactics

Military commanders deployed the streltsy in static formations, often against set formations or fortifications. They often fired from a platform and employed a mobile wooden "fortification" known in Russian as a "Gulyay-gorod" (literally a "walking fort"). They reportedly fired in volley or caracole fashion; the first line firing and then stepping back to reload while the second line stepped forward to fire.

Politics

At the end of the 16th century, there were 20,000-25,000 streltsy; in 1681, there were 55,000, including 22,500 in Moscow alone. Streltsy's engagement in handicrafts and trade led to a significant proprietary inequality among them and their blending with tradepeople. Even though Streltsy demonstrated their fighting efficiency on several occasions, such as the siege of Kazan in 1552, the war with Livonia, the Polish-Swedish invasion in the early 17th century and military operations in Poland and Crimea, in the second half of the 17th century Streltsy started to display their backwardness compared to the regular soldier or reiter regiments (see Regiments of the new type). Military service hardships, frequent salary delays, abuse on the part of local administration and commanders led to regular Streltsy's (especially the poorest ones) participation in anti-serfdom uprisings in the 17th and early

Streltsy in a famous paint by Sergey Ivanov 1864-1910

18th centuries, such as the peasant wars in the beginning of the 17th century and in 1670–1671 (leader – Stepan Razin), urban uprisings (Moscow Uprising of 1682, Streltsy Uprising of 1698, Astrakhan Uprising of 1705–1706).

At the same time, those streltsy who had been on top of the hierarchy enjoyed their social status and, therefore, tried to hold back the regular streltsy forces and keep them on the government's side. In the late 17th century, the streltsy of Moscow began to actively participate in a struggle for power between different government groups, supporting the Old Believers and showing hostility towards any foreign innovations.

The streltsy became something of a "praetorian element" in Muscovite politics in the late 17th century. In 1682 they attempted to prevent Peter the Great from coming to the throne in favor of his half-brother, Ivan.

Disbandment

After the fall of Sophia Alekseyevna in 1689, the government of Peter the Great engaged in a process of gradual limitation of the streltsy's military and political influence. Eight Moscow regiments were removed from the city and transferred to Belgorod, Sevsk, and Kiev.

In spite of these measures, the streltsy revolted yet again while Peter was on his Great Embassy in Europe. Although the revolt was put down by the Scottish general Patrick Gordon (he had entered Russian service under Tsar Alexei Mikhailovich in 1661) even before the Tsar's return to Russia, Peter nonetheless cut short his embassy and returned to finally crush the streltsy with savage reprisals, including public executions and torture. Tortures included roasting the bare back, tearing flesh with iron hooks, and crushing feet in wooden presses called butuks; executions included being broken on the wheel and being buried alive. Many of the bodies were hung around the monastery where Princess Sophia and Eudoxia were confined for aiding the rebellion.

The corps was technically abolished in 1689; however, after having suffered a defeat at Narva in 1700, the government stopped their disbandment. The most efficient streltsy regiments took part in the most important military operations of the Great Northern War and in Peter's Prut Campaign of 1711. Gradually, streltsy were incorporated into the regular army. At the same time, they started to disband the Municipal Streltsy.

Liquidation of most streltsy units was finally finished in the 1720s; however, the Municipal Streltsy were kept in some cities until the late 18th century.

The Preobrazhensky and Semenovsky regiments of Imperial Guards replaced the streltsy and the Ryndy as the tsar's bodyguards.

Historical portrait of Ivan IV, called the Terrible (1530-1584)

THE FIRST TZAR

IVAN THE TERRIBLE

Ivan IV Vasilyevich (25 August 1530 - 28 March 1584), commonly known as **Ivan the Terrible** or **Ivan the Fearsome**, (*Ivan Grozny*, with correct translation from Russian being *Ivan the Formidable*), was the Grand Prince of Moscow from 1533 to 1547, then "Tsar of All the Russias" until his death in 1584. The last title was used by all his successors.

During his reign, Russia conquered the Khanates of Kazan, Astrakhan and Sibir, becoming a multiethnic and multicontinental state spanning approximately 4,050,000 km². Ivan exercised autocratic control over Russia's hereditary nobility and developed a bureaucracy to administer his new territories. He transformed Russia from a medieval state into an empire, though at immense cost to its people, and its broader, long-term economy.

Historic sources present disparate accounts of Ivan's complex personality: he was described as intelligent and devout, yet given to rages and prone to episodic outbreaks of mental instability that increased with his age. In one such outburst, he killed his son and heir Ivan Ivanovich. This left his younger son, the pious but politically ineffectual Feodor Ivanovich, to inherit the throne.

Ivan was an able diplomat, a patron of arts and trade, and founder of the Moscow Print Yard, Russia's first publishing house. He was popular among Russia's commoners, except possibly the people of Novgorod and surrounding areas, and he is also noted for his paranoia and harsh treatment of the Russian nobility.

Sobriquet

The English word *terrible* is usually used to translate the Russian word *grozny* in Ivan's nickname, but this is a somewhat archaic translation. The Russian word *grozny* reflects the older English usage of *terrible* as in "inspiring fear or terror; dangerous; powerful; formidable". It does not convey the more modern connotations of English *terrible*, such as "defective" or "evil". Vladimir Dal defines *grozny* specifically in archaic usage and as an epithet for tsars: "courageous, magnificent, magisterial and keeping enemies in fear, but people in obedience".Other translations have also been suggested by modern scholars.

Early life

Ivan was the first son of Vasili III and his second wife, Elena Glinskaya, who was of half Serbian and half Russian descent. When Ivan was three years old, his father died from an abscess and inflammation on his leg that developed into blood poisoning. Ivan was proclaimed the Grand Prince of Moscow at the request of his father. His mother Elena Glinskaya initially acted as regent, but she died of what many believe to be assassination by poison, in 1538 when Ivan was only eight years old.

The regency then alternated between several feuding boyar families fighting for control. According to his own letters, Ivan, along with his younger brother Yuri, often felt neglected and offended by the mighty boyars from the Shuisky and Belsky families. In a letter to Prince Kurbski Ivan remembers, "They began to feed us as if we were foreigners or the most wretched menials. What sufferings did I not endure through lack of clothing and through hunger !"

On 16 January 1547, at age sixteen, Ivan was crowned with Monomakh's Cap at the Cathedral of the Dormition. He was the first to be crowned as "Tsar of All the Russias", hence claiming the ancestry of Kievan Rus'. Prior to that, rulers of Muscovy were crowned as Grand Princes, although Ivan III the Great, his grandfather, styled himself "tsar" in his correspondence.

Two weeks after his coronation, Ivan married his first wife Anastasia Romanovna, a member of the Romanov family, who became the first Russian tsaritsa.

By being crowned Tsar, Ivan was sending a message to the world and to Russia: he was now the one and only supreme ruler of the country, and his will was not to be questioned.

"The new title symbolized an assumption of powers equivalent and parallel to those held by former Byzantine Emperor and the Tatar Khan, both known in Russian sources as Tsar.

The political effect was to elevate Ivan's position." The new title not only secured the throne, but it also granted Ivan a new dimension of power, one intimately tied to religion. He was now a "divine" leader appointed to enact God's will, as "church texts described Old Testament kings as 'Tsars' and Christ as the Heavenly Tsar."

The newly appointed title was then passed on from generation to generation: "succeeding Muscovite rulers ... benefited from the divine nature of the power of the Russian monarch ... crystallized during Ivan's reign."

Domestic policy

Despite calamities triggered by the Great Fire of 1547, the early part of Ivan's reign was one of peaceful reforms and modernization. Ivan revised the law code, creating the Sudebnik of 1550, founded a standing army (the *streltsy*), established the Zemsky Sobor (the first Russian parliament of the feudal Estates type) and the council of the nobles, and confirmed the position of the Church with the Council of the Hundred Chapters (*Stoglavy Synod*), which unified the rituals and ecclesiastical regulations of the whole country. He introduced local self-government to rural regions, mainly in the northeast of Russia, populated by the state peasantry.

By Ivan's order in 1553 the Moscow Print Yard was established and the first printing press was introduced to Russia. Several religious books in Russian were printed during the 1550s and 1560s. The new technology provoked discontent among traditional scribes, leading to the Print Yard being burned in an arson attack. The first Russian printers, Ivan Fedorov and Pyotr Mstislavets, were forced to flee from Moscow to the Grand Duchy of Lithuania. Nevertheless, printing of books resumed from 1568 onwards, with Andronik Timofeevich Nevezha and his son Ivan now heading the Print Yard.

Ivan had St. Basil's Cathedral constructed in Moscow to commemorate the seizure of Kazan. Legend has it that he was so impressed with the structure that he had the architect, Postnik Yakovlev, blinded so that he could never design anything as beautiful again. In reality, Postnik Yakovlev went on to design more churches for Ivan and the walls of the Kazan Kremlin in the early 1560s, as well as the chapel over St. Basil's grave that was added to St. Basil's Cathedral in 1588, several years after Ivan's death. Although more than one architect was associated with this name and constructions, it is believed that the principal architect is one and the same person.

Other events of this period include the introduction of the first laws restricting the mobility of the peasants, which would eventually lead to serfdom, instituted during the rule of future tsar Boris Godunov in 1597.

Oprichnina

The 1560s brought hardships to Russia that led to dramatic change of Ivan's policies. Russia was devastated by a combination of drought and famine, unsuccessful wars against the Polish–Lithuanian Commonwealth, Tatar invasions and the sea-trading blockade carried out by the Swedes, Poles and the Hanseatic League. His first wife, Anastasia Romanovna, died in 1560, and her death was suspected to be a poisoning. This personal tragedy deeply hurt Ivan and is thought to have affected his personality, if not his mental health. At the same time, one of Ivan's advisors, Prince Andrei Kurbsky, defected to the Lithuanians, took command of the Lithuanian troops and devastated the Russian region of Velikiye Luki. The series of treasons made Ivan paranoically suspicious of nobility. On 3 December 1564, Ivan departed Moscow for Aleksandrova Sloboda. From there he sent two letters in which he announced his abdication because of the alleged embezzlement and treason of the aristocracy and clergy. The boyar court was unable to rule in Ivan's absence and feared the wrath of the Muscovite citizenry. A boyar envoy departed for Aleksandrova Sloboda to beg Ivan to return to the throne. Ivan agreed to return on condition of being granted absolute power. He demanded that he should be able to execute and confiscate the estates of traitors without interference from the boyar council or church. Upon this, Ivan decreed the creation of the oprichnina.

The oprichnina consisted of a separate territory within the borders of Russia, mostly in the territory of the former Novgorod Republic in the north. Ivan held exclusive power over the oprichnina territory. The Boyar Council ruled the zemshchina ('land'), the second division of the state. Ivan also recruited a personal guard known as the Oprichniki. Originally it was a thousand strong.

The oprichniki were headed by Malyuta Skuratov. One known oprichnik was the German adventurer Heinrich von Staden. The oprichniki enjoyed social and economic privileges under the oprichnina. They owed their allegiance and status to Ivan, not to heredity or local bonds.

The first wave of persecutions targeted primarily the princely clans of Russia, notably the influential families of Suzdal. Ivan executed, exiled or forcibly tonsured prominent members of the boyar clans on questionable accusations of conspiracy. Among those executed were the Metropolitan Philip and the prominent warlord Alexander Gorbaty-Shuisky. In 1566 Ivan extended the oprichnina to eight central districts. Of the 12,000 nobles there, 570 became oprichniks, the rest were expelled.

Under the new political system, the Oprichniki were given large estates, but unlike the previous landlords, could not be held accountable for their actions. These men "took virtually all the peasants possessed, forcing them to pay 'in one year as much as they used to pay in ten.' This degree of oppression resulted in increasing cases of peasants fleeing, which in turn led to a drop in the overall production. The price of grain increased by a factor of ten.

Sack of Novgorod

Conditions under Oprichnina were worsened by the 1570 epidemics of plague that killed 10,000 people in Novgorod. In Moscow it killed 600–1,000 daily. During the grim conditions of the epidemics, famine and ongoing Livonian War, Ivan grew suspicious that noblemen of the wealthy city of Novgorod were planning to defect, placing the city itself into the control of the Grand Duchy of Lithuania. In 1570 Ivan ordered the Oprichniki to raid the city. The Oprichniki burned and pillaged Novgorod and the surrounding villages, and the city was never to regain its former prominence.

Casualty figures vary greatly in different sources. The First Pskov Chronicle estimates the number of victims at 60,000. Yet the official death toll named 1,500 of Novgorod's *big* people (nobility) and mentioned only about the same number of *smaller* people. Many modern researchers estimate the number of victims to range from 2,000–3,000 (after the famine and epidemics of the 1560s the population of Novgorod most likely did not exceed 10,000–20,000). Many survivors were deported elsewhere.

Oprichnina did not live long after the sack of Novgorod. During the 1571–72 Russo-Crimean war, oprichniks failed to prove themselves worthy against a regular army. In 1572, Ivan abolished the Oprichnina and disbanded his oprichniks.

Foreign policy Diplomacy and trade

In 1547, Hans Schlitte, the agent of Ivan, recruited craftsmen in Germany for work in Russia. However, all these craftsmen were arrested in Lübeck at the request of Poland and Livonia.

The German merchant companies ignored the new port built by Ivan on the River Narva in 1550 and continued to deliver goods in the Baltic ports owned by Livonia. Russia remained isolated from sea trade.

Ivan established close ties with the Kingdom of England. Russo-English relations can be traced to 1551, when the Muscovy Company was formed by Richard Chancellor, Sebastian Cabot, Sir Hugh Willoughby and several London merchants. In 1553, Richard Chancellor sailed to the White Sea and continued overland to Moscow, where he visited Ivan's court. Ivan opened up the White Sea and the port of Arkhangelsk to the Company and granted the Company privilege of trading throughout his reign without paying the standard customs fees. Muscovy Company retained the monopoly in Russo-English trade until 1698.

With the use of English merchants, Ivan engaged in a long correspondence with Elizabeth I of England. While the queen focused on commerce, Ivan was more interested in a military alliance. During his troubled relations with the boyars, the tsar even asked her for a guarantee to be granted asylum in England should his rule be jeopardized. Elizabeth agreed on condition that he provided for himself during his stay.

Ivan IV corresponded with overseas Orthodox leaders. In response to a letter of Patriarch Joachim of Alexandria asking the Tsar for financial assistance for the Saint Catherine's Monastery in the Sinai Peninsula, which had suffered from the Turks, Ivan IV sent in 1558 a delegation to Egypt Eyalet by archdeacon Gennady, who, however, died in Constantinople before he could reach Egypt. From then on the embassy was headed by Smolensk merchant Vasily Poznyakov. Poznyakov's delegation visited Alexandria, Cairo and Sinai, brought the patriarch a fur coat and an icon sent by the Tsar and left an interesting account of its 2½ years of travels.

Conquest of Kazan and Astrakhan

While Ivan IV was a minor, armies of the Kazan Khanate repeatedly raided the northeast of Russia, In the 1530s the Crimean khan formed an offensive alliance with Safa Giray of Kazan, his relative. When Safa Giray invaded Muscovy in December 1540, the Russians used Qasim Tatars to contain him. After his advance was stalled near Murom, Safa Giray was forced to withdraw to his own borders.

These reverses undermined Safa Giray's authority in Kazan. A pro-Russian party, represented by Shahgali, gained enough popular support to make several attempts to take over the Kazan throne.

In 1545 Ivan IV mounted an expedition to the River Volga to show his support for pro-Russian factions. In 1551 the tsar sent his envoy to the Nogai Horde and they promised to maintain neutrality during the impending war. The Ar begs and Udmurts submitted to Russian authority as well.

In 1551 the wooden fort of Sviyazhsk was transported down the Volga from Uglich all the way to Kazan. It was used as the Russian *place d'armes* during the decisive campaign of 1552.

On 16 June 1552 Ivan IV led a 150,000-strong Russian army towards Kazan. The last siege of the Tatar capital commenced on 30 August. Under the supervision of Prince Alexander Gorbaty-Shuisky, the Russians used battering rams and a siege tower, undermining and 150 cannon. The Russians also had the advantage of efficient military engineers. The city's water supply was blocked and the walls were breached. Kazan finally fell on 2 October, its fortifications were razed, and much of the population massacred. About 60,000–100,000 Russian prisoners and slaves were released. The Tsar celebrated his victory over Kazan by building several churches with oriental features, most famously Saint Basil's Cathedral on Red Square in Moscow.

The fall of Kazan had as its primary effect the outright annexation of the Middle Volga. The Bashkirs accepted Ivan IV's authority two years later. In 1556 Ivan annexed the Astrakhan Khanate, destroyed the largest slave market on the Volga, and had a new fortress built on a steep hill overlooking the river. These conquests complicated the migration of the aggressive nomadic hordes from Asia to Europe through Volga. As a result of the Kazan campaigns, Muscovy was transformed into the multinational and multi-faith state of Russia.

Russo-Turkish war

In 1568, the Grand Vizier Sokollu Mehmet Paşa, who was the real power in the administration of the Ottoman Empire under Sultan Selim, initiated the first encounter between the Ottoman Empire and her future northern rival. The results presaged the many disasters to come. A plan to unite the Volga and Don by a canal was detailed in Constantinople. In the summer of 1569 a large force under Kasim Paşa of 1,500 Janissaries, 2,000 Spakhs, and few thousand Azaps and Akıncıs were sent to lay siege to Astrakhan and begin the canal works, while an Ottoman fleet besieged Azov.

Early in 1570, Ivan's ambassadors concluded a treaty at Constantinople that restored friendly relations between the Sultan and the Tsar.

Livonian War

In 1558 Ivan launched the Livonian War in an attempt to gain access to the Baltic Sea and its major trade routes. The war ultimately proved unsuccessful, stretching on for 24 years and engaging the Kingdom of Sweden, the Grand Duchy of Lithuania, the Polish–Lithuanian Commonwealth, and the Teutonic Knights of Livonia. The prolonged war had nearly destroyed the economy, while the *Oprichnina* had thoroughly disrupted the government. Meanwhile the Union of Lublin had united the Grand Duchy of Lithuania and Kingdom of Poland, and the Commonwealth acquired an energetic leader, Stefan Batory, who was supported by Russia's southern enemy, the Ottoman Empire. Ivan's realm was being squeezed by two of the great powers of the time.

After rejected peace proposals from his enemies, Ivan IV found himself in a difficult position by 1579. The displaced refugees fleeing the war compounded the effects of the simultaneous drought, and exacerbated war engendered epidemics, causing much loss of life.

Batory then launched a series of offensives against Muscovy in the campaign seasons of 1579–81, trying to cut the Kingdom of Livonia from Muscovite territories. During his first offensive in 1579, he retook Polotsk with 22,000 men. During the second, in 1580, he took Velikie Luki with a 29,000-strong force. Finally, he began the Siege of Pskov in 1581 with a 100,000-strong army. Narva in Estonia was reconquered by Sweden in 1581.

Unlike Sweden and Poland, Denmark under Frederick II had trouble continuing the fight against Muscovy. He came to an agreement with John III of Sweden, in 1580, transferring the Danish titles of Livonia to John III. Muscovy recognized Polish–Lithuanian control of Livonia only in 1582. After Magnus von Lyffland, brother of Fredrick II and former ally of Ivan, died in 1583, Poland invaded his territories in the Duchy of Courland, and Frederick II decided to sell his rights of inheritance. Except for the island of Saaremaa, Denmark was out of the Baltic by 1585.

Crimean raids

In the later years of Ivan's reign, the southern borders of Muscovy were disturbed by Crimean Tatars. Their main purpose was the capture of slaves. Khan Devlet I Giray of Crimea repeatedly raided the Moscow region. In 1571, the 40,000-strong Crimean and Turkish army launched a large-scale raid. Due to the ongoing Livonian War, Moscow's garrison was as small as 6,000, and could not even delay the Tatar approach. Unresisted, Devlet devastated unprotected towns and villages around Moscow and caused the 1572, Fire of Moscow. Historians estimate the number of casualties of the fire from 10,000 to as many 80,000 people.

To buy peace from Devlet Giray, Ivan was forced to relinquish his claims on Astrakhan in favor of the Crimean Khanate. This defeat angered Ivan. Between 1571 and 1572, preparations were made upon his orders. In addition to Zasechnaya cherta, innovative fortifications were set beyond the River Oka that defined the border.

The following year, Devlet launched another raid on Moscow, now with a 120,000-strong horde, equipped with cannons and reinforced by Turkish janissaries. On 26 July 1572, the horde crossed the River Oka near Serpukhov, destroyed the Russian vanguard of 200 noblemen and advanced towards Moscow.

The Russian army, led by Prince Mikhail Vorotynsky, was half the size, estimated at between 60,000–70,000 men; yet it was an experienced streltsi army, equipped with modern firearms and gulyay-gorods. On 30 July the armies clashed near the River Lopasnya in what would be known as the Battle of Molodi, which continued for more than a week. The outcome was a decisive Russian victory.

The Crimean horde was defeated so thoroughly that both the Ottoman Sultan and the Crimean khan, his vassal, had to give up their ambitious plans of northward expansion into Russia.

Conquest of Siberia

During Ivan's reign, Russia started a large-scale exploration and colonization of Siberia. In 1555, shortly after the conquest of Kazan, the Siberian khan Yadegar and the Nogai Horde under Khan Ismail pledged their allegiance to Ivan, in hope that he would help them against their opponents.

However, Yadegar failed to gather the full sum of tribute he proposed to the tsar, so Ivan did nothing to save his inefficient vassal. in 1563 Yadegar was overthrown and killed by Khan Kuchum, who denied any tribute to Moscow.

In 1558 Ivan gave the Stroganov merchant family the patent for colonising "the abundant region along the Kama River", and in 1574, lands over the Ural Mountains along the rivers Tura and Tobol. They also received permission to build forts along the Ob and Irtysh rivers. Around 1577, the Stroganovs engaged the Cossack leader Yermak Timofeyevich to protect their lands from attacks of the Siberian Khan Kuchum.

In 1580 Yermak started his conquest of Siberia. With some 540 Cossacks, he started to penetrate territories that were tributary to Kuchum. Yermak pressured and persuaded the various family-based tribes to change their loyalties and become tributaries of Russia. Some agreed voluntarily, under better terms than with Kuchum; others were forced. He also established distant forts in the newly conquered lands. The campaign was successful, and the Cossacks managed to defeat the Siberian army in the Battle of Chuvash Cape, but Yermak was still in need for reinforcements. He sent an envoy to Ivan the Terrible, with a message that proclaimed Yermak-conquered Siberia a part of Russia, to the dismay of the Stroganovs, who had planned to keep Siberia for themselves. Ivan agreed to reinforce the Cossacks with his streltsi. Yermak's conquest expanded Ivan's empire to the east and allowed him to style himself "Tsar of Siberia" in the tsar's very last years.

▲ A Russian Streltsy

Death

Ivan died from a stroke while playing chess with Bogdan Belsky on 28 March 1584. Upon Ivan's death, the Russian throne was left to his unfit and childless middle son Feodor. Feodor died childless in 1598, ushering in the Time of Troubles.

FEODOR I OF RUSSIA

Fyodor (Theodore) I Ivanovich or **Feodor I Ioannovich** 31 May 1557 – 16/17 January 1598), also known as **Feodor the Bellringer,** was the last Rurikid Tsar of Russia (1584–1598).

Feodor's mother died when he was three, and he grew up in the shadow of his father, Ivan the Terrible. A pious man of retiring disposition, Feodor took little interest in politics, and the country was effectively administered in his name by Boris Godunov, the brother of his beloved wife Irina. His childless death left the Rurikid dynasty extinct, and spurred Russia's descent into the catastrophic Time of Troubles.

Background

Feodor was born in Moscow, the son of Ivan IV (The Terrible) by his first wife Anastasia Romanovna. Although he was the sixth and youngest child of his mother, he grew up with only one older brother, Ivan, because all his other older siblings died before Feodor was one year old. His mother also died by the time Feodor was three years old, and her death greatly affected his father, who had been very attached to his wife. Ivan the Terrible began to earn his sobriquet 'the terrible' during the years of Feodor's childhood. He also took a series of other wives, but Feodor's only surviving half-sibling, Dmitry of Uglich, was fully twenty-five years younger than him.

Feodor therefore grew up in the shadow of a terrible father, with no mother to succor him, and only his older brother Ivan for family solidarity. He grew to be sickly of health and diffident of temperament. He was extremely pious by nature, spending hours in prayer and contemplation. He was very fond of visiting churches, and would often cause the bells to be rung according to a special tradition in the Russian Orthodox Church. For this reason, he is known to history as **Feodor the Bellringer.** Overall, he was considered a good-natured, simple-minded man who took little interest in politics. By some reports, he may have suffered from intellectual disability or learning disability, but this may have been a misinterpretation of his nature and behavior.

Marriage

In 1580, Feodor married Irina (Alexandra) Feodorovna Godunova (1557 – 26 October/23 November 1603), sister of Ivan's minister Boris Godunov. Although the marriage was arranged by the Tsar, and the couple knew nothing of each other before their wedding day, they went on to have a strong marriage. The lonely Feodor soon grew extremely close to his wife, to a degree that was unusual for that period and milieu. Husband and wife shared a relationship of warmth and trust which was the support of Feodor's life as long as he lived. However, the marriage was not immediately blessed with children, and may not have even been consummated for some years. It was only in 1592, after almost twelve years of marriage, that Tsaritsa Irina gave birth to a daughter, who was named Feodosia after her father. Feodor and his wife doted on their daughter, who however died aged two in 1594. There were no other children from the marriage.

In November 1581, Feodor's elder brother Ivan Ivanovich was killed by their father in a fit of rage. His death meant that Feodor became the heir to his father's throne. He had never been considered a candidate for the Russian throne until that moment, and was not a little daunted by the prospect. One year later, in October 1582, his father's latest wife bore a son, Dmitry of Uglich, who was Feodor's only surviving sibling. Ivan the Terrible died in March 1584, and Feodor became Tsar. Two months later, on 31 May 1584, he was crowned Tsar and Autocrat of all Russia at Assumption Cathedral in Moscow.

Feodor was only the nominal ruler: his wife's brother and trusted minister Boris Godunov legitimized himself, after Ivan IV's death, as a de facto regent for the weak and disabled Feodor. Feodor's failure to sire other children brought an end to the centuries-old central branch of the Rurik dynasty. Feodor was succeeded as tsar by Godunov. The termination of the dynasty can also be considered to be one of the reasons for the Time of Troubles. He died in Moscow and was buried at Archangel Cathedral, Kremlin.

Foreign policy

Unlike his father, Feodor had no enthusiasm for maintaining exclusive trading rights with the Kingdom of England. Feodor declared his kingdom open to all foreigners, and dismissed the English ambassador Sir Jerome Bowes, whose pomposity had been tolerated by Feodor's father. Elizabeth I sent a new ambassador, Giles Fletcher, the Elder, to demand of Boris Godunov that he convince the tsar to reconsider. The negotiations failed because Fletcher addressed Feodor with two of his titles omitted. Even after this setback, Elizabeth continued to address Feodor on that topic in half appealing, half reproachful letters. She proposed an alliance between Russia and England, something which she had refused to do when it had been sought by Feodor's father, but he turned her down.

BORIS GODUNOV

Boris Fyodorovich Godunov (c. 1551 – 23 April 1605) ruled the Tsardom of Russia as *de facto* regent from c. 1585 to 1598 and then as the first non-Rurikid tsar from 1598 to 1605. The end of his reign saw Russia descend into the Time of Troubles.

Early years

Boris Godunov was the most noted member of an ancient, now extinct, Russian family of Tatar origin (Chet), which came from the Horde to Kostroma in the early 14th century. This legend is written in the annals dating from early 17th century. He was descended from the Tatar Prince Chet, who went from the Golden Horde to Russia and founded the Ipatiev Monastery in Kostroma. Boris was the son of Feodor Ivanovich Godunov "Krivoy" ("the one-eyed") (died, c. 1568–1570) and his wife Stepanida Ivanovna. His older brother Vasily died young and without issue.

Godunov's career began at the court of Ivan the Terrible. He is mentioned in 1570 for taking part in the Serpeisk campaign being an archer of the guard. The following year, he became an oprichnik – a member of Ivan's personal guard and secret police. In 1570/1571, Godunov strengthened his position at court by his marriage to Maria Grigorievna Skuratova-

▲ The Tzar Boris Fyodorovich Godunov

Belskaya, the daughter of oprichniks' head Malyuta Skuratov-Belskiy.

In 1580, the Tsar chose Boris Godunov's sister Irina Godunova (1557 – 26 October/23 November 1603) to be the wife of his second son and eventual heir, the fourteen-year-old Feodor Ivanovich (1557–1598). On this occasion, Godunov was promoted to the rank of *Boyar*. On 15 November 1581, he was present at the scene of the Tsar's murder of his own eldest son, the crown prince Ivan. Godunov tried to intervene, but received blows from the Tsar's sceptre. The elder Ivan immediately repented and Godunov rushed to get help for the Tsarevich, who died four days later.

Three years later, on his deathbed, Ivan IV appointed a council consisting of Godunov, Feodor Nikitich Romanov, Vasili Shuiski and others, to guide his son and successor of Russia Feodor I, who was feeble both in mind and body: "he took refuge from the dangers of the palace in devotion to religion; and though his people called him a saint, they recognized that he lacked the iron to govern men." Upon his death, Ivan also left the three-year-old Dmitry Ivanovich (1581–1591), from his seventh and last marriage. Since the Orthodox Church recognized legitimate only his first three marriages, and any offspring thereof, Dmitri (and his mother's family) had no claim to the throne. Still, taking no chances, shortly after Ivan's death the Council had both Dmitri and his mother Maria Nagaya moved to Uglich, some 120 miles north of Moscow. It was there in 1591 that Dmitri died at the age of ten.

As Dmitri's death was announced by the church bell, the people of Uglich rose up in protest against what they suspected was an assassination commissioned by Boris Godunov. Troops were sent and the rebellion was swiftly quelled. Then Boris Godunov ordered the Uglich bell clapper – "tongue" – to be removed, the bell to be flogged in public and sent to exile in Siberia along with the townspeople who had not been executed.

An official commission headed by Vasili Shuiski was sent to determine the cause of death. The official verdict was that the boy had cut his throat during an epileptic seizure. Ivan's widow claimed that her son had been murdered by Godunov's agents. Godunov's guilt was never established and shortly thereafter Dmitri's mother was forced to take the veil. Dmitry Ivanovich was laid to rest and promptly, though temporarily, forgotten.

Regency

At the coronation of Feodor Ivanovich as Tsar Feodor I on 31 May 1584, Boris received honors and riches as a member of the regency council, in which he held the second place during the life of the Tsar's uncle Nikita Romanovich. When Nikita died in 1586, Boris had no serious rival for the regency. A conspiracy of other boyars and of Dionysius II, Metropolitan of Moscow, sought to break Boris's power by divorcing the Tsar from Godunov's childless sister. The attempt proved unsuccessful, and the conspirators were banished or sent to monasteries. After that, Godunov remained supreme in Russia and he corresponded with foreign princes as their equal.

His policy was generally pacific and always prudent. In 1595, he recovered from Sweden some towns lost during the former reign. Five years previously he had defeated a Tatar raid upon Moscow, for which he received the title of *Konyushy*, an obsolete dignity even higher than that of *Boyar*. He supported an anti-Turkish faction in the Crimea and gave the emperor subsidies in his war against the sultan.

Godunov encouraged English merchants to trade with Russia by exempting them from duties. He built towns and fortresses along the north-eastern and south-eastern borders of Russia to keep the

Tatar and Finnic tribes in order. These included Samara, Saratov, Voronezh, and Tsaritsyn, as well as other lesser towns. He colonized Siberia with scores of new settlements, including Tobolsk.

During his rule, the Russian Orthodox Church received its patriarchate, placing it on an equal footing with the ancient Eastern churches and freeing it from the influence of the Patriarch of Constantinople. This pleased the Tsar, as Feodor took a great interest in church affairs.

In Godunov's most important domestic reform, a 1597 decree forbade peasants to transfer from one landowner to another, thus binding them to the soil. This ordinance aimed to secure revenue, but it led to the institution of serfdom in its most oppressive form.

Reign

On the death of the childless Feodor on 7 January 1598, self-preservation as much as ambition led Boris to seize the throne. Had he not done so, the mildest treatment he could have hoped for would have been lifelong seclusion in a monastery. His election was proposed by Patriarch Job of Moscow, who believed that Boris was the one man capable of coping with the difficulties of the situation. Boris, however, would accept the throne only from the Zemsky Sobor (national assembly) which met on 17 February and unanimously elected him on 21 February. On 1 September, he was solemnly crowned tsar.

During the first years of his reign, he was both popular and prosperous, and ruled well. He recognized the need for Russia to catch up with the intellectual progress of the West and did his best to bring about educational and social reforms. He was the first tsar to import foreign teachers on a large scale, the first to send young Russians abroad to be educated, and the first to allow Lutheran churches to be built in Russia. After the Russo–Swedish War (1590–1595), he pursued gaining access to the Baltic Sea and attempted to obtain Livonia by diplomatic means. He cultivated friendly relations with the Scandinavians and hoped to take a bride from a foreign royal house, thereby increasing the dignity of his own dynasty. However he declined the personal union proposed to him in 1600 by the diplomatic mission led by Lew Sapieha from the Polish-Lithuanian Commonwealth.

Boris died after a lengthy illness and a stroke on 13/23 April 1605. He left one son, Feodor II, who succeeded him and ruled for only a few months, until he and Boris' widow were murdered by the enemies of the Godunovs in Moscow on 10/20 June 1605. Boris's first son, Ivan, was born in 1587 and died in 1588. His daughter, Xenia, was born in 1582. She was engaged to Johann of Schleswig-Holstein, but he died shortly before their planned wedding in October 1602. Xenia was given the name "Olga" upon being forced to take monastic vows at the Voskesesnskij Monastery in Beloozero and her name is inscribed as "the Nun Olga Borisovna" at the crypt of the Godunovs at the Trinity Lavra of St. Sergius where she lived from 1606, when she sojourned there to attend the reburial of her father, until her death in 1622. Boris, his wife, and their children are buried together in a mausoleum near the entrance of the Assumption Cathedral at Trinity-St. Sergius Lavra.

FYODOR II

Borisovich Godunov of Russia (1589 – 1605) was a tsar of Russia (1605) during the Time of Troubles. He was born in Moscow, the son and successor to Boris Godunov. His mother Maria Grigorievna Skuratova-Belskaya was one of the daughters of Malyuta Skuratov, the infamous favourite of Ivan the Terrible. Physically robust and passionately beloved by his father, he received the best education available at that time, and from childhood was initiated into all the minutiae of government, besides sitting regularly in the council and receiving the foreign envoys. He seems also to have been remarkably and precociously intelligent, creating a map of Russia, which is still preserved. It was edited with some additions by Hessel Gerritsz in Amsterdam, in 1613, and had been reedited until 1665.

On the sudden death of Boris the sixteen-year-old was proclaimed tsar (13 April 1605). Though his father had taken the precaution to surround him with powerful friends, he lived from the first moment of his reign in an atmosphere of treachery. On 11 June (N. S.) 1605 the envoys of False Dmitriy I arrived at Moscow to demand his removal, and the letters which they read publicly in Red Square decided his fate. A group of boyars, unwilling to swear allegiance to the new tsar, seized control of the Kremlin and arrested him.

On 10 or 20 June Feodor was strangled in his apartment, together with his mother. Officially, he was declared to have been poisoned, but the Swedish diplomat Peter Petreius stated that the bodies, which had been on public display, showed traces of a violent struggle. Although aged 16 at best, Feodor was known to be physically strong and agile and it took four men to overpower him.

DMITRY I

Dmitry I was the Tsar of Russia from 10 June 1605 until his death on 17 May 1606. He is sometimes referred to as **False Dmitry I**.

He was the first, and most successful, of three "impostors" who claimed during the Time of Troubles to be the youngest son of Ivan the Terrible, tsarevich Dmitry Ivanovich, who had supposedly escaped a 1591 assassination attempt. It is generally believed that the real Dmitry died in Uglich, and that this Dmitry's name was actually **Grigoriy Otrepyev**, although this is far from certain.

Background

Dmitry I entered history circa 1600, after making a positive impression on Patriarch Job of Moscow with his learning and assurance. Upon hearing of this, Tsar Boris Godunov ordered the young man to be seized and examined, whereupon Dmitry fled to Prince Constantine Ostrogski at Ostroh, of the Polish–Lithuanian Commonwealth, and subsequently entered the service of the Wisniowieckis, a polonized Ruthenian family. Two family members in particular, the princes Adam and Michał Wiśniowiecki, were intrigued by the stories Dmitry told of whom he purported to be, as it gave the Poles real opportunity to capitalize on the political rancor rising in Moscow.

There were rumors that Dmitry was an illegitimate son of the Polish king, Stefan Batory, who had reigned from 1575 to 1586; according to a later tale, Dmitry blurted out that identity when once slapped by a violent master. Dmitry's own story was that the Tsar Ivan's widow his mother, anticipating Boris Godunov's assassination attempt, had given the young tsarevich into the care of a doctor, who placed him in various Russian monasteries through the years. After the doctor's death, Dmitry had then fled to Poland, working there as a teacher for a brief time, before being accepted into the service of the Wisniowieckis. Several of those who had known Ivan IV claimed later that Dmitry did indeed resemble the young tsarevich; further, the young man also displayed aristocratic tendencies, such as horsemanship and literacy, and was fluent in Russian, Polish, and French.

However, regardless of whether or not Dmitry's tale was authentic, the Wiśniowiecki brothers, along with Samuel Tyszkiewicz, Jan Sapieha, Roman Różyński, and several other Polish noblemen soon agreed to fully back the man, and his claim, against Tsar Boris Godunov. In March 1604, Dmitry visited the royal court of Sigismund III Vasa in Kraków. The king provisionally supported him, but gave no promise of military aid to help ease the young man's path to the throne. To attract the support of powerful Jesuits in lieu of the king outright stating anything, Dmitry publicly converted to Roman Catholicism on 17 April 1604, thus convincing papal nuncio Claudio Rangoni to also back up the young Russian's claim. During his time at court, Dmitry met Marina Mniszech, daughter of the Polish nobleman Jerzy Mniszech. Dmitry and Marina fell in love; asking her father for her hand, the young man was promised it in return for granting the Mniszechs full rights to the Russian towns of Pskov, Novgorod, Smolensk, and Novhorod-Siverskyi upon his ascension.

Way to the Russian throne

When Boris Godunov received word of Dmitry's Polish support, he spread claims of the younger man being just a runaway monk called Grigory Otrepyev, although on what information these claims were based is unproven. Regardless, the tsar's public support soon began to wane, especially as Dmitry's loyalists spread counter-rumors. Several Russian boyars also pledged themselves to Dmitry, thus giving them a "legitimate" reason not to pay taxes to Tsar Boris.

Dmitry, having now gained the full support of the Polish Commonwealth, formed a small army of approximately 3,500 soldiers from various private forces. With these men, he advanced on Russia in March 1605. Godunov's many enemies, including the southern Cossacks, joined Dmitry's army on the long march to Moscow. Thus combined, these forces fought two engagements with reluctant Russian soldiers; winning the first, they captured Chernigov (modern *Chernihiv*), Putivl (*Putyvl*), Sevsk, and Kursk, but they badly lost the second battle, almost to the point of disintegrating.

The young man's cause was only saved when news of the sudden death of Boris Godunov on 13 April 1605 reached his troops in the aftermath.

With the unpopular tsar dead, the last impediment to Dmitry's progress had been swept away; the victorious Russian troops defected to Dmitry's side, followed soon by others, swelling the Polish ranks as they marched further in. Finally, on 1 June, the disaffected boyars of Moscow staged a palace coup, imprisoning newly crowned tsar Feodor II and his mother, the widow of Boris Godunov.

On 20 June, Dmitry made his triumphal entry into Moscow, and on 21 July, he was crowned tsar by a new Muscovite Patriarch of his own choosing, the Greek Patriarch Ignatius.

The new tsar moved to consolidate his power by visiting the tomb of Tsar Ivan, and the convent of his widow Maria Nagaya, who accepted him as her son and "confirmed" his story. The Godunovs, including Tsar Feodor and his mother, were executed, with the exception of Tsarevna Xenia, whom Dmitry took as his royal concubine for five months. In contrast to Godunov's policies, many of the noble families Tsar Boris had exiled – such as the Shuiskys, Golitsins and Romanovs – were granted the pardon of Tsar Dmitry and allowed to return to Moscow. Feodor Romanov, sire of the future imperial dynasty, was soon appointed as metropolitan of Rostov; old patriarch Job, who did not recognize the new tsar, was sent into exile.

Dmitry planned to introduce a series of political and economical reforms. He restored Yuri's Day, the day when serfs were allowed to move to another lord, to ease the conditions of peasantry. His favorite at the Russian court, the 18-year-old Prince Ivan Khvorostinin, is considered by historians to be one of Russia's first Westernizers.

In foreign policy, Dmitry sought an alliance with his sponsor, the Polish Commonwealth, and the Papal States. He planned for war against the Ottoman Empire, ordering the mass production of firearms to serve in the conflict. In his correspondence, he referred to himself as "Emperor of Russia" a century before Tsar Peter I used the title, though this was not recognized at the time. Dmitry's royal depictions featured him clean-shaven, with slicked-back dark hair; an unusual look for the era. On 8 May 1606, Dmitry married Marina Mniszech in Moscow. It was the usual practice that when a Russian Tsar married a woman of another faith, she would convert to Eastern Orthodox Christianity. Rumors circulated that Dmitry had obtained the support of the Polish king Sigismund and Pope Paul V by promising to reunite the Russian Orthodox Church and the Holy See; it was for these alleged reasons, claimed the rumors, that Tsarina Marina did not convert to the Orthodox faith. This angered the Russian Orthodox Church, the boyars, and the population alike.

The resentful Prince Vasily Shuisky, head of the boyars, began to plot against the tsar, accusing Dmitry of spreading Roman Catholicism, Lutheranism, and sodomy. This gained popular support, especially as Dmitry surrounded himself with foreigners who flouted Russian customs. According to Russian chronicler Avraamy Palitsyn, Dmitry further enraged many Muscovites by permitting his Catholic and Protestant soldiers, whom the Russian Church regarded as heretics, to pray in Orthodox churches. Shuisky's adherents had spread word that Tsar Dmitry was about to order his Polish retainers to lock the city gates and massacre the people of Moscow. Whether such orders existed or not, Palitsyn's chronicle reported them as undeniable fact.

Death

On the morning of 17 May 1606, ten days after Dmitry's marriage to Tsarina Marina, a massive number of boyars and commoners stormed the Kremlin. Tsar Dmitry tried to flee, jumping out a window, but fractured his leg in the fall. He fled to a bathhouse and attempted to disappear within, but was recognized and dragged out before the populace by the boyars, who killed the tsar lest he successfully muster an appeal to the crowd. His body was put on display and then cremated, with the ashes allegedly shot from a cannon towards Poland. According to Palitsyn, Dmitry's death was followed by the massacre of his supporters. Palitsyn boasted in his chronicle that, "a great amount of heretical blood was spilled on the streets of Moscow."

Dmitry's reign had lasted a mere eleven months. Prince Shuisky then took his place as Tsar Vasili IV of Russia. However, two further impostors later appeared, False Dmitry II and False Dmitry III, the first of whom was publicly "accepted" by Tsarina Marina as her fallen husband.

VASILI IV OF RUSSIA

Vasili IV of Russia (22 September 1552 – 12 September 1612) was Tsar of Russia between 1606 and 1610 after the murder of False Dmitriy I. His reign fell during the Time of Troubles. He was the only member of House of Shuysky to become Tsar and the last member of the Rurikid dynasty to rule.

He was a son of Ivan Andreyevich Shuisky. Born Prince Vasili Ivanovich Shuisky, he was descended from sovereign princes of Nizhny Novgorod and a 20th generation male line descendant of the Varangian prince Rurik. He was one of the leading boyars of Tsardom of Russia during the reigns of Feodor I and Boris Godunov. In all the court intrigues of the Time of Troubles, Vasily and his younger brother Dmitry Shuisky usually acted together and fought as one.

It was he who, in obedience to the secret orders of Tsar-to-be Boris, went to Uglich to inquire into the cause of the death of the Tsarevich Dmitry Ivanovich, the youngest son of Ivan the Terrible, who had perished there in mysterious circumstances. Shuisky reported that it was a case of suicide, though rumors abounded that the Tsarevich had been assassinated on the orders of the regent

▲ The Tzar Vasili IV

Boris Godunov. Some suspected that Dmitry escaped the assassination and that another boy was killed in his place, providing impetus for the repeated appearance of impostors. On the death of Boris, who had become tsar, and the accession of his son Feodor II, Shuisky went back upon his own words in order to gain favour with the pretender False Dmitriy I, who was attempting to gain the throne by impersonating the dead Tsarevich. Shuisky recognized the pretender as the "real" Dmitry despite having earlier determined the boy had committed suicide, thus bringing about the assassination of the young Feodor.

Shuisky then conspired against the false Dmitriy and brought about his death (May 1606). After stating publicly that the real Dmitriy had indeed been slain and that the reigning tsar was an impostor, Shuisky's adherents thereupon proclaimed him tsar on 19 May 1606. He reigned until 19 July 1610, but was never generally recognized. Even in Moscow itself he had little or no authority, and he only avoided deposition by the dominant boyars because they had no one to replace him with. The popularity of his cousin, Prince Mikhail Skopin-Shuisky, who commanded an army aided by a small allied Swedish army led by Jacob de la Gardie, demanding cessions of Russian territory in Karelia in return, allowed Shuisky, for a time, to remain on his unstable throne. In 1610, he was deposed by his former adherents Princes Vorotynsky and Mstislavsky. He was made a monk and eventually transported together with his two brothers to Warsaw by the Polish hetman Stanisław Żółkiewski. He died a prisoner in the castle of Gostynin, near Warsaw, in 1612, followed soon by his brother Dmitry. There they were forced to perform the Shuysky Tribute before the Polish King and Senate. The Romanovs, elected in 1613, did recognize Vasili posthumously as a legal tsar, and during their negotiations with the Polish authorities constantly demanded the right to rebury his body in Russia. Following the Treaty of Polyanovka in 1635, Vasili's remains were finally returned to Moscow and laid to rest in the Archangel Cathedral.

Marriages and issue

Vasili Shuisky was married twice. His first wife, Elena Mikhailovna Repnina, died prior his election to tsardom, and he had no children from that marriage. After his coronation, Vasili remarried Princess Ekaterina Buynosova-Rostovskaya, whose name was changed to Maria, deemed more suitable for a tsarina consort. They had two daughters together, Princesses Anna and Anastasia of all the Russias, but both died in infancy during their father's reign, and were buried in the Old Maiden's Convent in Kremlin. As both brothers of Vasili, Princes Dmitri Shuisky and Ivan Shuisky the Button, died also childless, the Shuiskys' princely house became extinct after the death of the latter in 1638.

THE LAST TZAR BEFORE PETER THE GREAT

Michael I of Russia (22 July 1596 – 23 July 1645) became the first Russian Tsar of the house of Romanov after the zemskiy sobor of 1613 elected him to rule the Tsardom of Russia.

Aleksey Mikhailovich (29 March 1629 – 8 February January] 1676) was the Russian Tsar during some of Russia's most eventful decades in the mid-17th century. His reign saw wars with Poland and Sweden, schism in the Russian Orthodox Church and the major Cossack revolt of Stenka Razin.

Feodor (Theodore) III Alexeyevich of Russia (9 June 1661 – 7 May 1682) was the Tsar of all Russia between 1676 and 1682.

Ivan V Alekseyevich (6 September 1666 – 8 February 1696) was a joint Tsar of Russia (with his younger half-brother **Peter I**) who co-reigned between 1682 and 1696. He was the youngest son of Alexis I of Russia by his first wife Maria Miloslavskaya, while Peter was the only son of Alexis by his second wife Natalya Naryshkina. Ivan's reign was only formal, since he had serious physical and mental disabilities. He sat still for hours at a time and needed assistance in order to walk...

▲ A scene from the uprising: Natalia Naryshkina shows Ivan V to the Streltsy in order to prove that he is alive and well, while Patriarch Joachim of Moscow attempts to calm the crowd.

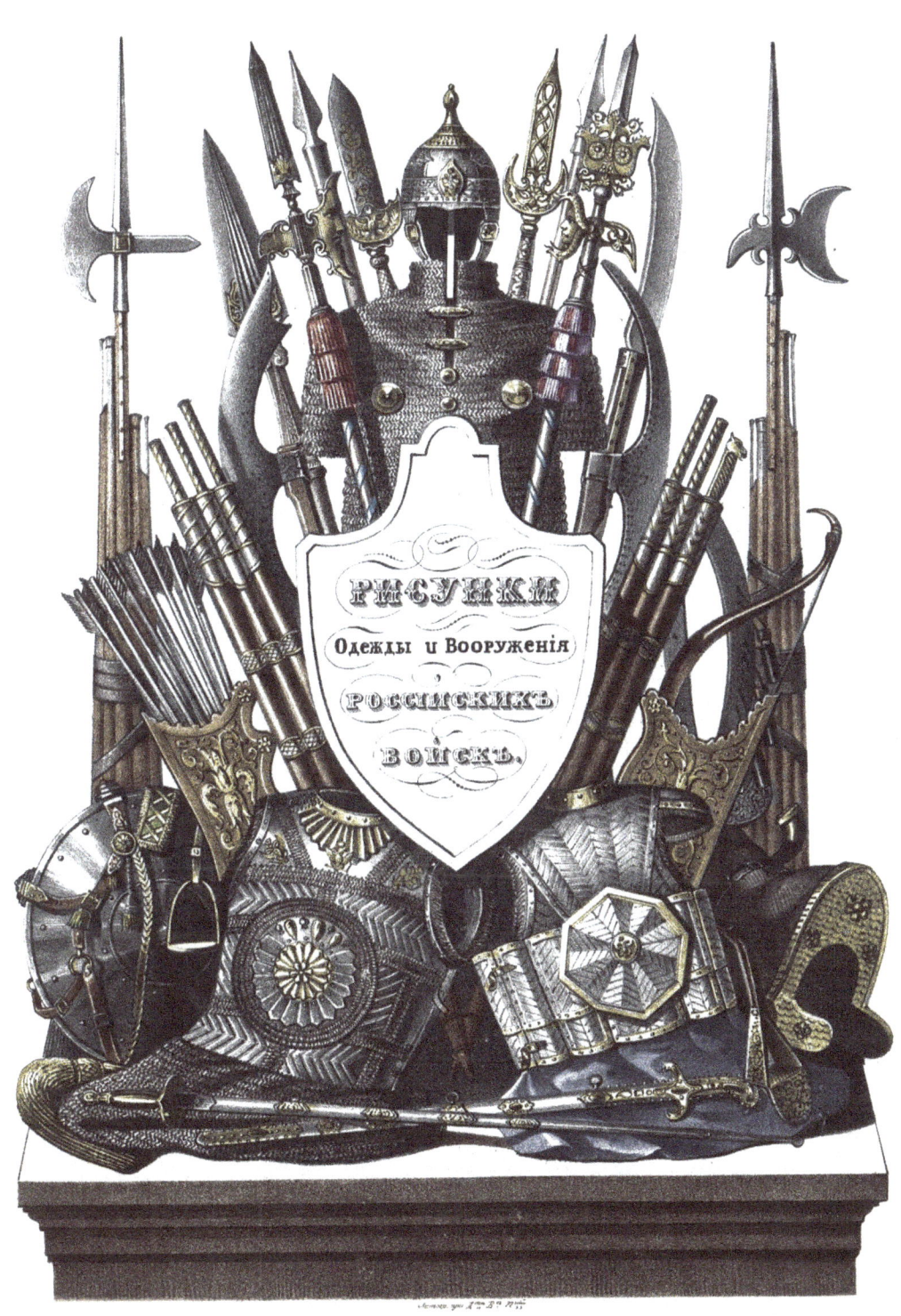

PLATES LIST OF ILLUSTRATIONS

People's Civil Clothing from 862 to 1700. Armament of the Provisional Troops. Clothing and armament of indispensable troops. Music. Banners. Signs of distinction. Attire or Artillery.

01 - Tsar Ivan Vasilyevich the Terrible. From the portrait of the Academy of Sciences in the Kunstkamor.
02 - Tsar Feodor Ioannovich. From the portrait of the Academy of Sciences in the Kunstkamor.
03 - Tsar Vasily Ivanovich Shuisky. From the portrait of the Academy of Sciences in the Kunstkamor.
04 - Tsar Boris Feodorovich Godunov. From the portrait of the Academy of Sciences in the Kunstkamor.
05 - Tsar Mikhail Feodorovich. From the portrait of the Academy of Sciences in the Kunstkamor.
06 - Tsar Theodore Alekseevich. From a portrait available in the Imperial Hermitage.
07 - Tsar Alexei Mikhailovich. From a portrait available in the Imperial Hermitage.
08 - Tsar John Alexeevich. From a portrait available in the Imperial Hermitage.

1 - Image of Grand Duke Vasily Ioannovich.
2 - Image of Tsar Feodor Ioannovich on Tsar Cannon in Moscow.
3 - Russian clothing in the XI century, prostonarodnaya cloth.
4 - Russian clothing in the XI century, Princes' Clothing.
5 - Russian clothing in the XI century, Princes' Clothing.
6 - Russian clothing in the XIV to the XVIII century, SOROCHKA.
7 - Russian clothes in the XIV to the XVIII century, the named sermyag and shapka.
8 - Russian clothes in the XIV to the XVIII century, KAFTAN AND SHAPKA. (The view depicts the city of Torzhok, at the beginning of the 17th century).
9 - Russian clothing in the XIV to the XVIII century, Ferez and Shapa.
10 - Russian clothing in the XIV to the XVIII century, the OXOBEN AND THE SHAPE.
11 - Russian clothing in the XIV to the XVIII century, single tuffy and shape. (The view depicts the Patriarchal-Village of Copper, near Tver, in the XVII century).
12 - Russian clothes in the XIV to the XVIII century, RUSSIAN SHUBA AND SHAPKA.
13 - Russian clothes in the XIV to the XVIII century, tursky oven and gorlain shapes. (A view depicts the city of Saratov at the beginning of the 17th century).
14 - Russian clothing in the XIV to the XVIII century, the Polish shank and shloe Gorlatna. (The species depicts part of the city of Pskov in the 17th century).
15 - Russian clothes in the XIV to the XVIII century, terlik and mashman shap. (A view of the city of Astrakhan at the beginning of the 17th century).
16 - Russian clothing in the 14th to the 18th century, the turkish caftaan and the murmolka shap. (The view depicts part of the Kolomna Palace of Tsar Alexei Mikhailovich).
17 - Russian clothes in the XIV to the XVIII century, zipun, tafia and shapka.
18 - Russian clothes in the XIV to the XVIII century, stain caftane and short gorlatnaya. (The view depicts the interior of a smaller golden chamber, in the Moscow Kremlin Palace, in the second half of the 17th century).
19 - Russian clothing in the XIV to the XVIII century, paid and a shoestring. (The view depicts part of the Moscow Kremlin and the Armory of that time).
20 - Image of Tsar Mikhail Feodorovich in the crazy, with the necklace and in the shape, belonging to the clothes of the Russian Sovereigns from the 14th to the 18th century.
21 - CONCEALING, from the XIV to XIII century.
22 - CONCEALING from the 14th to the 18th century.

23 - Russian by shelve, xiii century.

24 - Russian armament in the X and XI centuries, FANS OF WAR.

25 - Russian armament in the X and XI centuries, the horse warrior.

26 – 27 Russian armament from the fourteenth to the second half of the 17th century, pancier and kolchuga. bandana and bakhterets.

28 – 29 Russian arms from the XIV to the second half of the XVII century. bagter and colonary. jushman.

30 - Russian arms from the XIV to the second half of the XVII century. COOKY.

31 -32 -Russian arms from the XIV to the second half of the XVII century. THE MIRROR.

33 -34- Russian arms from the XIV to the second half of the XVII century. THE MIRROR.

35 - 36 - Russian arms from the XIV to the second half of the XVII century. barmitsa, zarukavye and the garment. wrapping.

37 - Russian arms from the XIV to the second half of the XVII century. MITTEN.

38 - Russian arms from the XIV to the second half of the XVII century. BUTTURLISHES.

39 - Russian arms from the XIV to the second half of the XVII century. BUTTURLISHES.

40 - Russian arms from the XIV to the second half of the XVII century. BUTTURLISHES.

41 - Russian arms from the XIV to the second half of the XVII century. MITTEN.

45 - Russian arms from the XIV to the second half of the XVII century. SHELOMS.

46 - Russian arms from the XIV to the second half of the XVII century. THE SHELMES.

47 - Russian arms from the XIV to the second half of the XVII century. COLPACKS.

48 - Russian arms from the XIV to the second half of the XVII century. Shishaki.

49 - Russian arms from the XIV to the second half of the XVII century. Shishaki.

50 - Russian arms from the XIV to the second half of the XVII century. MISSIONS-HABITS.

51 - Russian arms from the XIV to the second half of the XVII century. MISSERS-PAPERS.

52 - Russian arms from the XIV to the second half of the XVII century. PAPER WRAPPERS.

53 - Russian arms from the XIV to the second half of the XVII century. SHEARS IRON.

54 - Russian arms from the XIV to the second half of the XVII century. SHAPKA COPPER.

55 - Russian arms from the XIV to the second half of the XVII century. ERICHONICS.

56 - 57 Russian arms from the XIV to the second half of the XVII century. SHIELDS.

58 - 59 Russian arms from the XIV to the second half of the XVII century. SHIELDS.

60 - Russian arms from the XIV to the second half of the XVII century. POINT.

61 - 62 Russian arms from the XIV to the second half of the XVII century. swords

63 - 64 Russian arms from the XIV to the second half of the XVII century. palas, kon?ar and tesak. kniving blades, kinzhal, knives: subsecured and fittings.

65 - Russian arms from the XIV to the second half of the XVII century. SPEED, JIDES AND CLEAN.

66 – 67 Russian arms from the XIV to the second half of the XVII century. ROGATINA AND SOLDIER.

68 – 69 Russian arms from the XIV to the second half of the XVII century. BERDISHI. THE TOPORS.

70 – 71 Russian arms from the XIV to the second half of the XVII century. THE TOPORICS. CHECKS.

72 – 73 Russian arms from the XIV to the second half of the XVII century. SHESTOPERA. BULAVI.

74 - 75 Russian arms from the XIV to the second half of the XVII century. Ax and Blow.

76 - Accessories for weapons from the XIV to the second half of the XVII century. TOHTOI.

77 - Accessories for weapons from the XIV to the second half of the XVII century. Pokrovets on Saadak.

78 – 79 Russian arms from the XIV to the second half of the XVII century. SELF-LINES.

80 - Accessories for weapons from the XIV to the second half of the XVII century. A wine puddle.

81 - Russian firearms from the XIV to the second half of the XVII century. SAMAPALS OR HANDS.

82 - Russian firearms from the XIV to the second half of the XVII century. SAMAPALS OR HANDS.

83 - Russian firearms from the XIV to the second half of the XVII century. CARBINES.

84 - Russian firearms from the XIV to the second half of the XVII century. CARBINES.

85 – 86 Russian firearms from the 14th to the second half of the 17th century, PISTOLS. Firearms in the XVII century, pictures with toxor and pistols with toxors.

87 – 88 Accessories for firearms in the XV, XVI and XVII centuries, the Berendeyki. Accessories for armament from the XV to XVIII centuries, NATRUSKI.

89 - Accessories for armament from the XV to XVII centuries. NATURUSKI.

90 - Russian armament of the XVII century. alebards and partizans.

91 - Accessories to the Russian armament in the XVII century. prairpers.

92 Russian arms from the XIV to the second half of the XVII century. the principles in the tegilies and the shapes of the irons.

93 - Russian arms from the XIV to the second half of the XVII century. the prince in bakhters and in shishak with elite. (The view depicts a part of Novgorod, in the XVI century).

94 - Russian arms from the XIV to the second half of the XVII century. the battery and the shelm.

95 - Russian arms from the XIV to the second half of the XVII century. the case with the barmitz and the paper shape.

96 - Russian arms from the XIV to the second half of the XVII century. printers in yushmanah and in shishaka.

97 - Russian arms from the XIV to the second half of the XVII century. Warrior in Yushman and in Misyurka.

98 - Russian arms from the XIV to the second half of the XVII century. the harmony in the kuyak and the hair of the copper.

99 - Russian arms from the XIV to the second half of the XVII century. The Warrior in the Mirror and in the Sleeve. (The view depicts part of the Moscow Kremlin in the XVII century).

100 - Russian arms from the XIV to the second half of the XVII century. voevoda in two pancreas and in erihonk. (A view depicts the ancient Neuhausen Castle in Livonia).

101 - Russian arms from the XIV to the second half of the XVII century. voevoda in the mirror in the wire and in the erihonk.

102 - BOYARIN in the XVI and XVII centuries. (The view depicts part of the Kremlin from the side of Moskvorechye).

103 - Rynda in the XVI and XVII centuries.

104 - THE LIVING IN 1674.

105 - Horseradish in 1678.

106 - Streltsy in 1613. (The view depicts the Church of St. Basil the Blessed and the Kremlin wall in Moscow, at the beginning of the 17th century).

107 - MINE IN 1613. (The view depicts the courtyard before the former embassy home in Moscow).

108 - Streltsy of the Moscow Strelets' Regiments Lutokhin and Ivan Poltev: in 1674.

109 - Streltsy S of the Moscow Streletsky Regiments: Kolobov, Aleksandrov, Golovlinsky and Bukhvostov; In 1674.

110 - Streltsy of the Moscow Strelets Regiments: Lagowskin, Vorontsov and Naramansky; In 1674.

111 - Streltsy of the Moscow Strelets Regiments: Lagowskin, Vorontsov and Naramansky; In 1674.

112 - Standarbearer and Streltsy of the moscow streetsky Levshin regiment, in 1674.

113 - Initial people or officers of the Moscow Streletsky Regiments: in 1674.

114 - Armament of the pedestrian German regiments, who were in the Russian service in the XVII century; Shown in the Military Charter of 1647-th year.

115 – German musketeer of a regiments, who were in the Russian service in the XVII century

116 - German pikeman of a regiments, who were in the Russian service in the XVII century

117 -118 Musical instruments, used before the XVIII century in the armies of Foreign European States and serves as an explanation for the ancient. Tulumbas from the Wax and Pipes, XVI and XVII centuries.

119 - Famous Grotes used before 1700.

120 - Banner of the Tsar Ioann Vasilyevich Grozny, 1560.

121 - The banner of Prince Pozharsky, 1612.

122 - The banner of Prince Pozharsky, 1612.

123 - The Banner of Time of Tsar Alexei Mikhailovich, 1645-1676.

124 - Banner of 1645-1676 years.

125 - Banner of 1645-1676 years.

126 - The banners of the Moscow Streletsky Regiments in 1674.

127 - Banner of the year 1690.

128 - Banner of the year 1690.

129 - The banner of the reign of Tsar Peter Alekseevich, 1696-1699.

130 - Banner of 1696-1699 years.

131 - Banner of the Astrakhan Streltsy, 1693-th year.

132 - Banner of the Astrakhan Streltsy 1693-th year.

133 - The Banner of 1696.

134 - Banner of the Moscow Streltsy, 1699th year.

135 - Banner of the XVII century.

136 - Prapor XVII century.

137 - Prapor XVII century.

138 - Prapor XVII century.

139 - 2 pounds. Pischal, 1485 and 1/4 poods. Gafunitsa, 1542-th years.

140 – 141 - 5 1/2 lbs. Piscal, 1563 and 68 pounds. Inbrog Pischal, 1577

142-143 - 120 poods. Shotgun-King Cannon, 1586 year. 6 1/2 poods. Mortire, 1587 year.

144 – 145 - 52 lbs. Troil Peephal, 1590 and 38 pounds. Bear Piscal, 1590.

146 - 21 poods Mortyra, 1605-th year.

147 - 1 pound. Piscal, 1618 and 3/4 pound. Pishchal, 1666th

148-149 - 70 lbs. Pischal Unicorn, 1670th and 2 pounds. Pishchal, 1672 year. 2 pounds. Pishchal, 1673-th year and 2-pound Pishchal, 1674-th year.

150-151 - 20 lbs. Nightshade of Tsar Alexei Mikhailovich, 1645-1676 2-and 3-pound forged iron piches of the 16th and 17th centuries.

152-153 - 6 lbs. Wolf Pile, 1679 and 2 pounds. Pischal, 1679 year. 2 pounds. Pishchal, 1680th and 2-pound Pishchal, 1681 year.

154-155-156 - Zhagra or the Pintle of the XVII century. 50 lbs. Pischal, 1685 and 40 pounds. Parsal of Persia, 1686th year. 6 lbs. Gamayun Piscal, 1690th and 40 pound Cannon Eagle, 1692

Tsar Ivan Vasilyevich the Terrible. From the portrait of the Academy of Sciences in the Kunstkamor.

02

Tsar Feodor Joannovich. From the portrait of the Academy of Sciences in the Kunstkamor.

Tsar Vasily Ivanovich Shuisky. From the portrait of the Academy of Sciences in the Kunstkamor.

Tsar Boris Feodorovich Godunov. From the portrait of the Academy of Sciences in the Kunstkamor.

Tsar Mikhail Feodorovich. From the portrait of the Academy of Sciences in the Kunstkamor.

Tsar Theodore Alekseevich. From a portrait available in the Imperial Hermitage.

Tsar Alexei Mikhailovich. From a portrait available in the Imperial Hermitage.

Tsar John Alexeevich. From a portrait available in the Imperial Hermitage.

Image of Grand Duke Vasily Joannovich. - Image of Tsar Feodor Joannovich on Tsar Cannon in Moscow

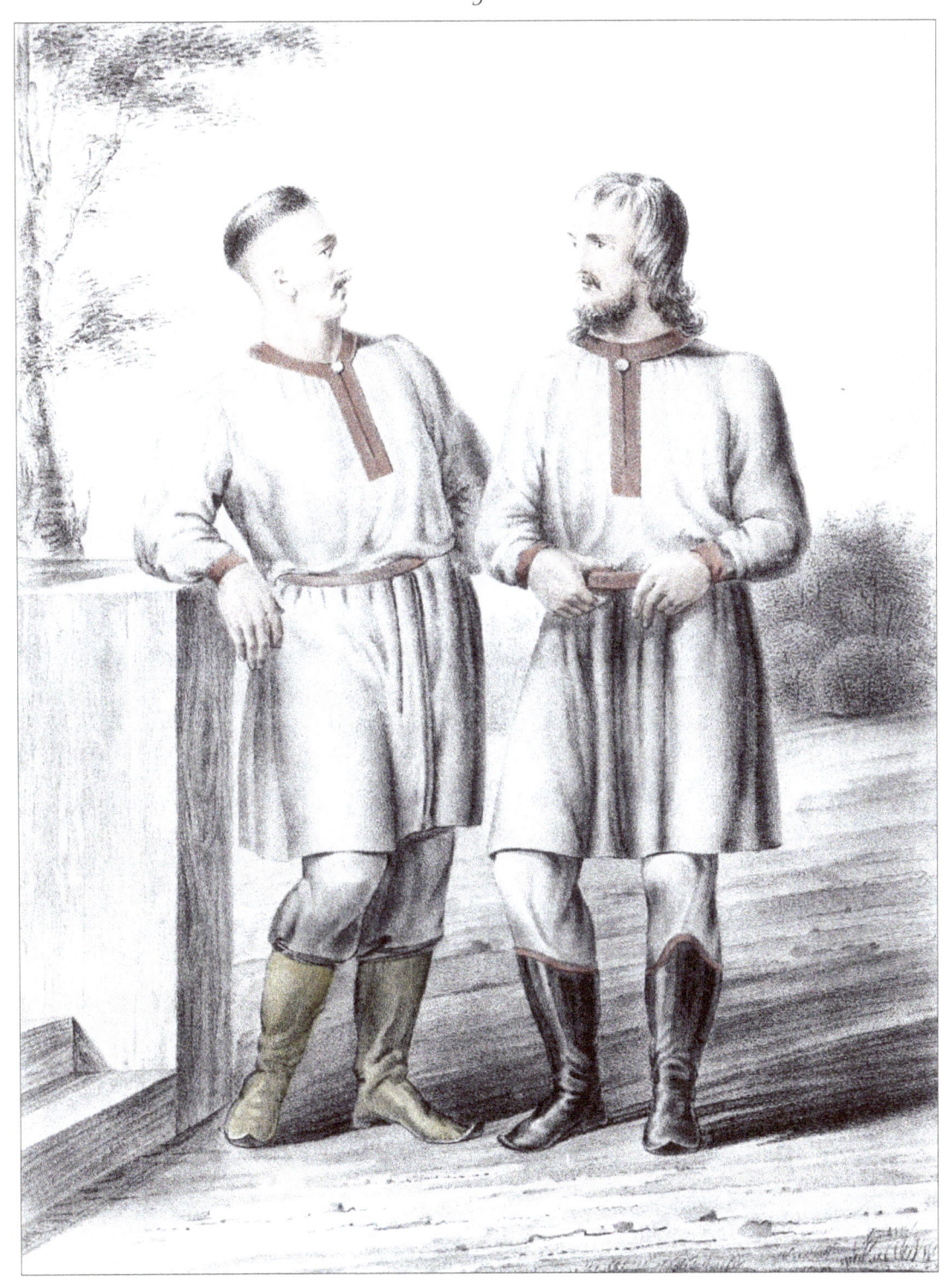

Russian clothing in the XI century, prostonarodnaya cloth.

Russian clothing in the XI century, Princes' Clothing.

Russian clothing in the XI century, Princes' Clothing.

Russian clothing in the XIV to the XVIII century, SOROCHKA.

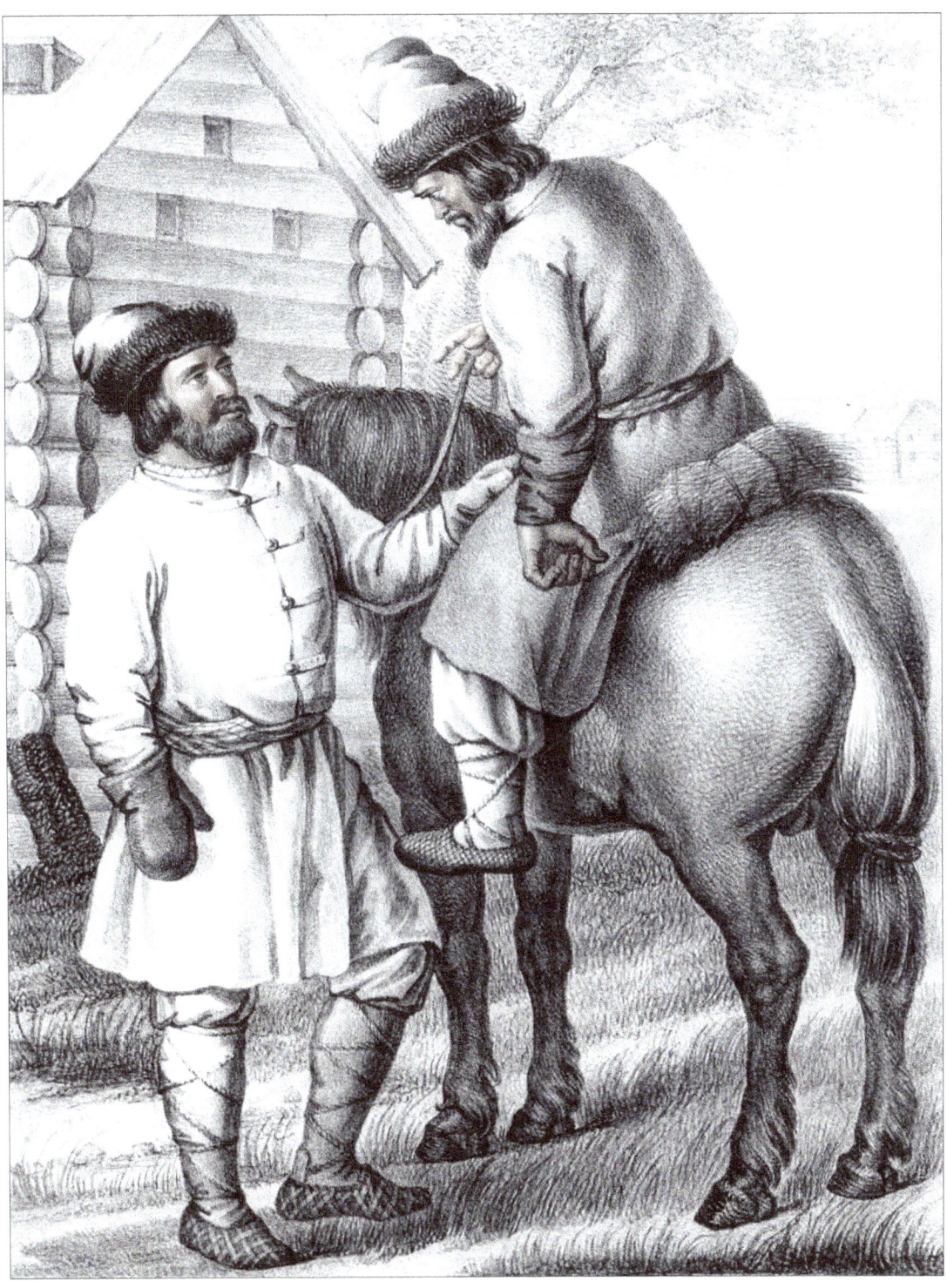

Russian clothes in the XIV to the XVIII century, the named sermyag and shapka.

Russian clothes in the XIV to the XVIII century, KAFTAN AND SHAPKA. (The view depicts the city of Torzhok, at the beginning of the 17th century).

Russian clothing in the XIV to the XVIII century, Ferez and Shapa.

Russian clothing in the XIV to the XVIII century, the oxoben and the shape.

Russian clothing in the XIV to the XVIII century, single tuffy and shape. (The view depicts the
Patriarchal-Village of Copper, near Tver, in the XVII century).

Russian clothes in the XIV to the XVIII century, russian shuba and shapka.

Russian clothes in the XIV to the XVIII century, tursky oven and gorlain shapes.

Russian clothing in the XIV to the XVIII century, the Polish shank and shloe Gorlatna.

Russian clothes in the XIV to the XVIII century, terlik and mashman shap.

Russian clothing in the 14th to the 18th century, the turkish caftaan and the murmolka shap.
(The view depicts part of the Kolomna Palace of Tsar Alexei Mikhailovich).

Russian clothes in the XIV to the XVIII century, zipun, tafia and shapka.

Russian clothes in the XIV to the XVIII century, stain caftane and short gorlatnaya.

Russian clothing in the XIV to the XVIII century, paid and a shoestring

Image of Tsar Mikhail Feodorovich in the crazy, with the necklace and in the shape, belonging to the clothes of the Russian Sovereigns from the 14th to the 18th century.

Russian by shelve, xiii century.

Concealing, from the XIV to XIII century.

Concealing from the 14th to the 18th century

Russian armament in the X and XI centuries, Fans Of War

Russian armament in the X and XI centuries, the horse warrior.

Russian armament from the fourteenth to the second half of the 17th century, pancier and kolchuga, bandana and bakhterets.

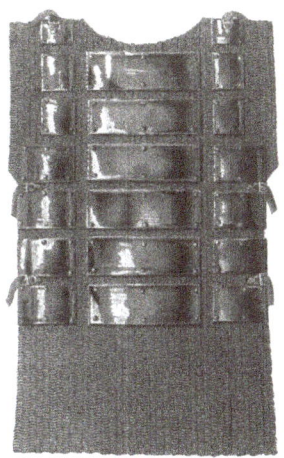

Russian arms from the XIV to the second half of the XVII century. bagter and colonary, jushman.

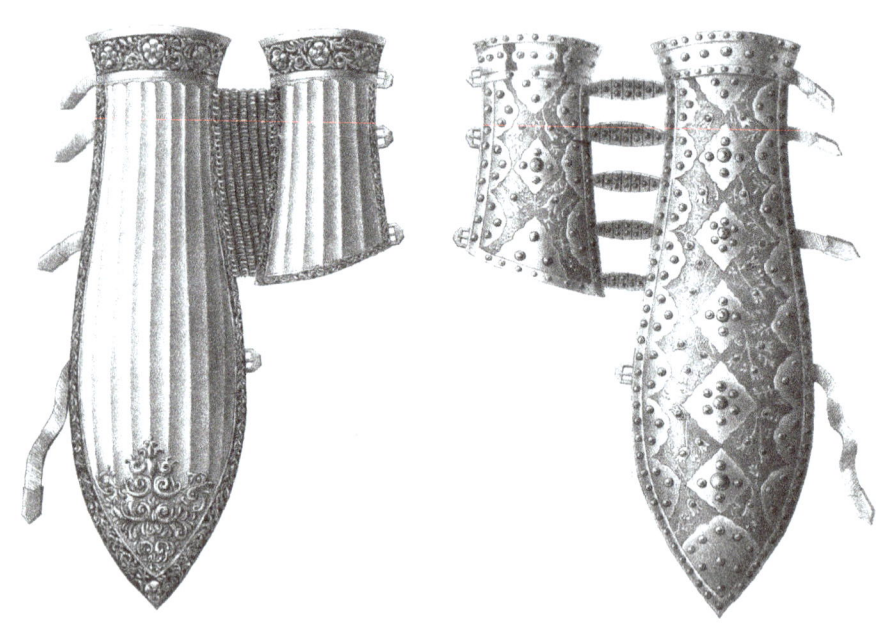

Russian arms from the XIV to the second half of the XVII century. cooky..

Russian arms from the XIV to the second half of the XVII century. the mirror.

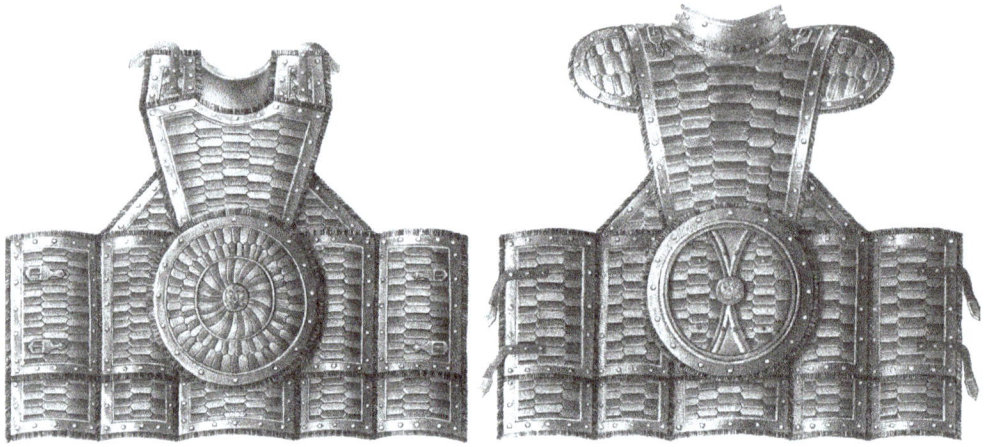

Russian arms from the XIV to the second half of the XVII century. the mirror.

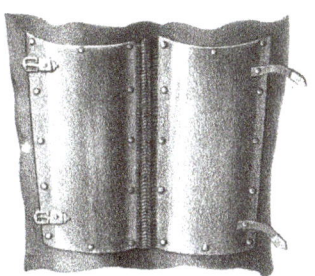

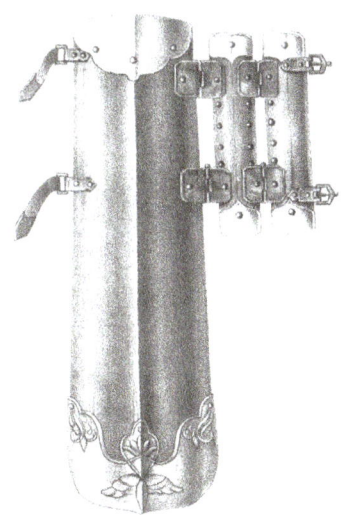

Russian arms from the XIV to the second half of the XVII century. barmitsa, zarukavye and the garment. wrapping

Russian arms from the XIV to the second half of the XVII century

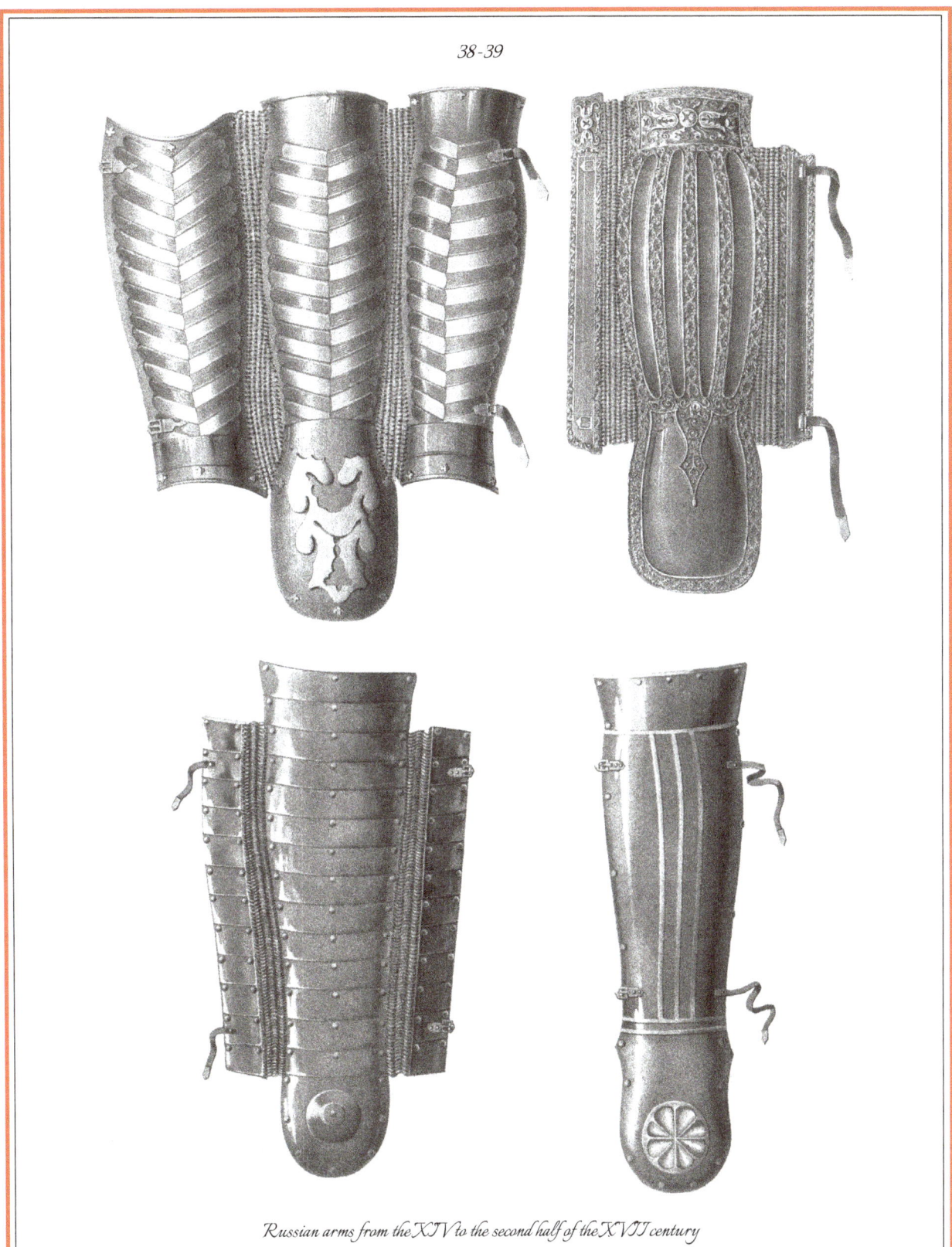

Russian arms from the XIV to the second half of the XVII century

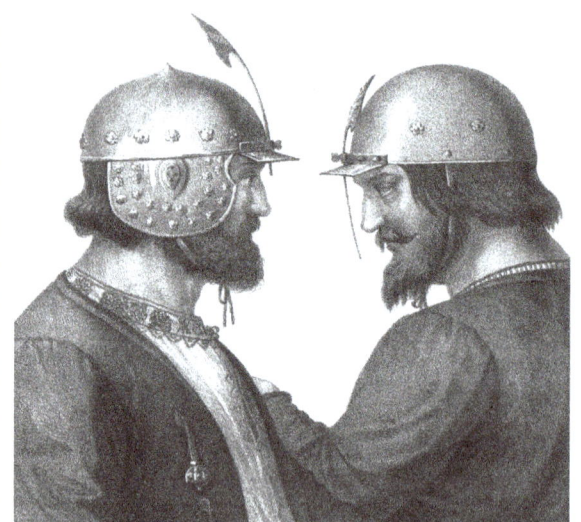
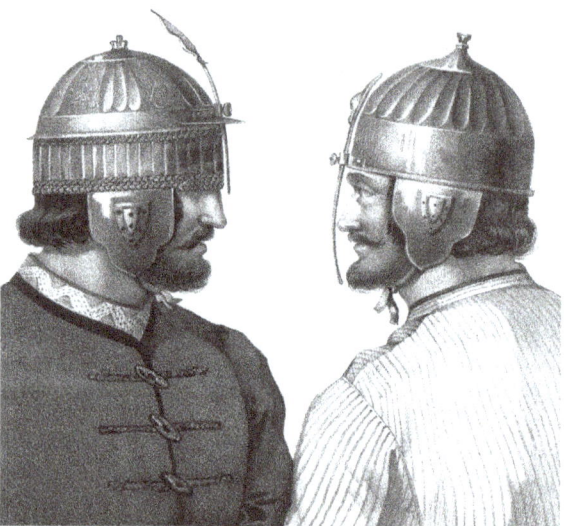

Russian arms from the XIV to the second half of the XVII century. Headgears and helmes

Russian arms from the XIV to the second half of the XVII century. Headgears and helmes

Russian arms from the XIV to the second half of the XVII century. Headgears and helmes

Russian arms from the XIV to the second half of the XVII century. Shields.

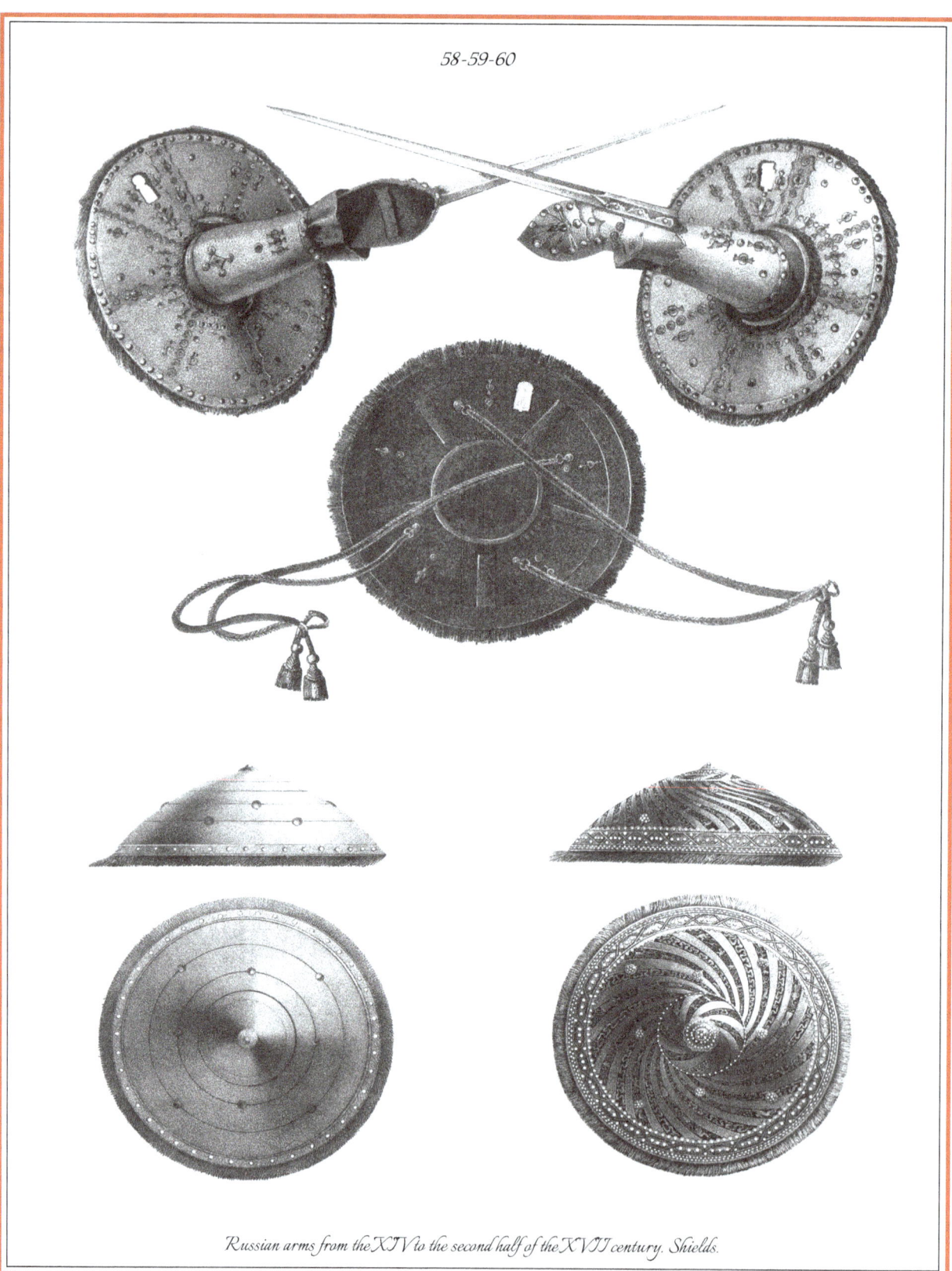

Russian arms from the XIV to the second half of the XVII century. Shields.

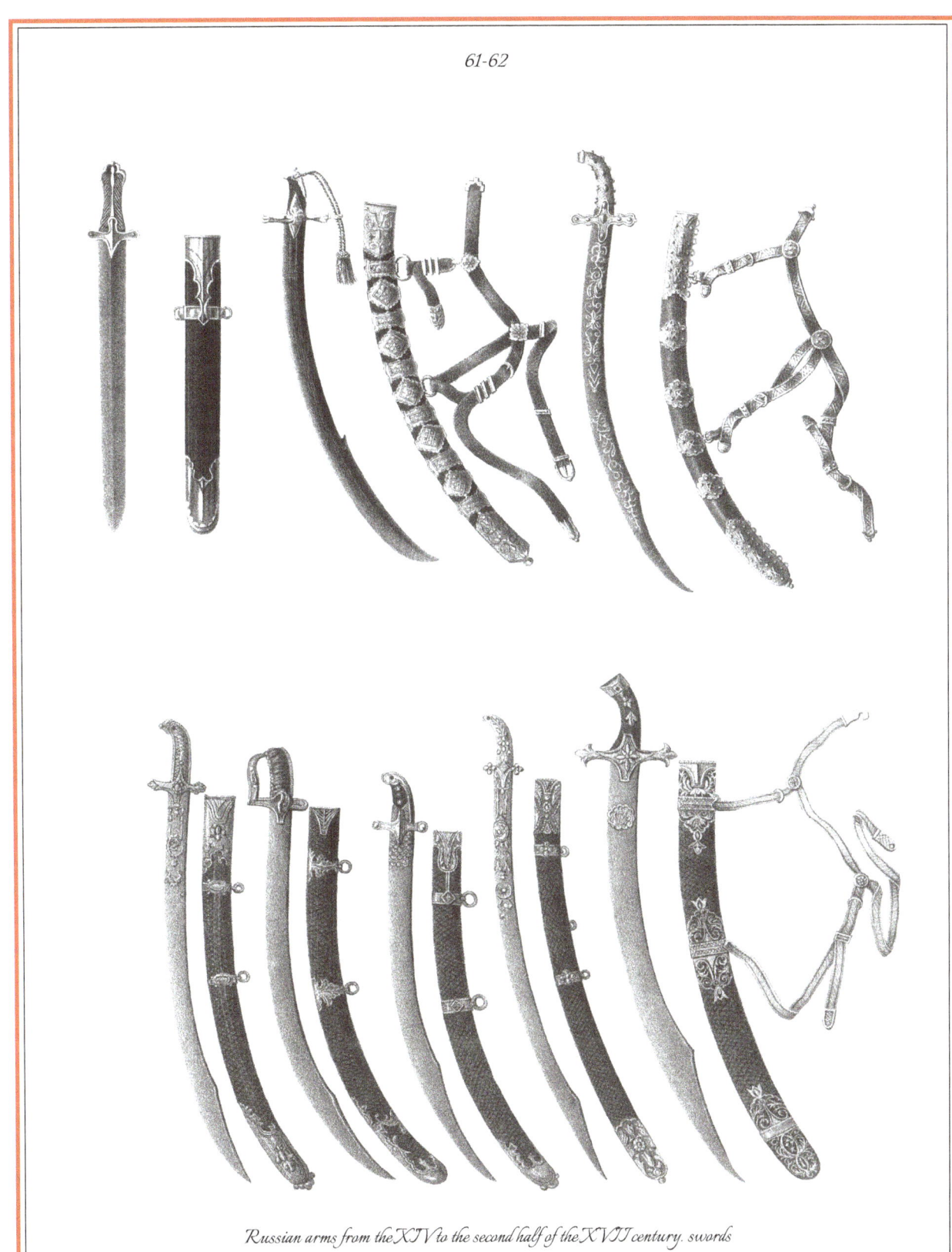

Russian arms from the XIV to the second half of the XVII century. swords

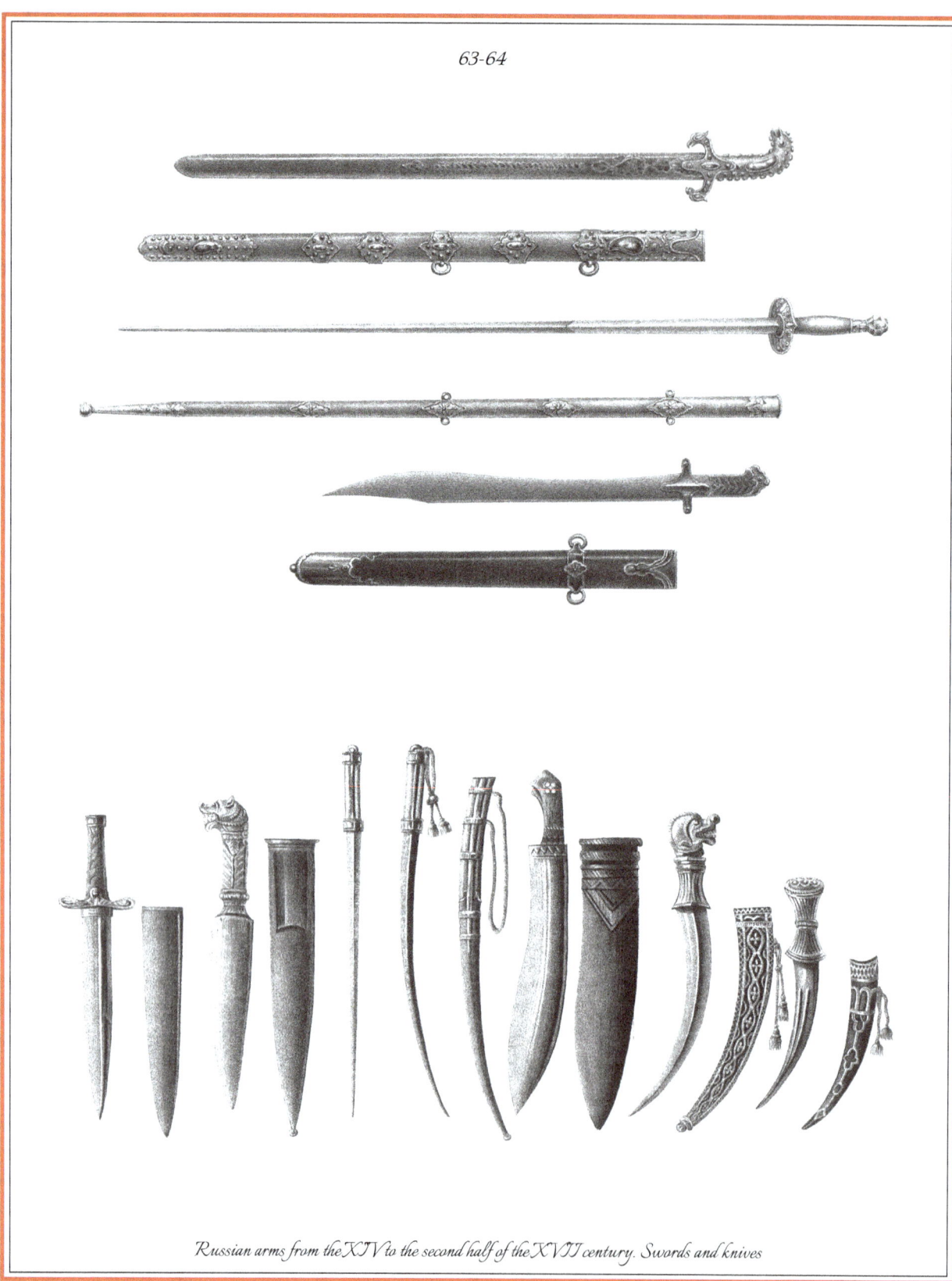

Russian arms from the XIV to the second half of the XVII century. Swords and knives

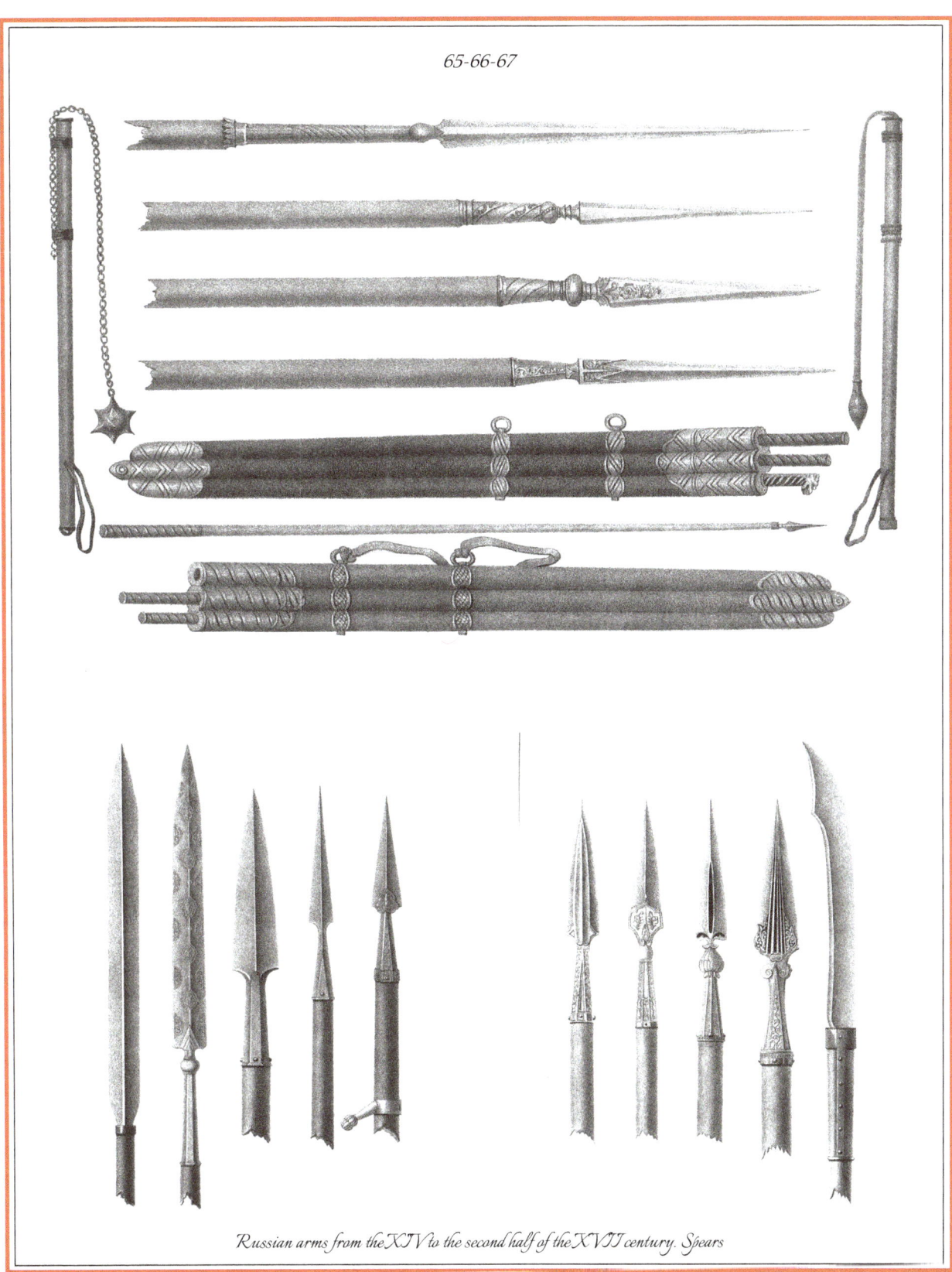

Russian arms from the XIV to the second half of the XVII century. Spears

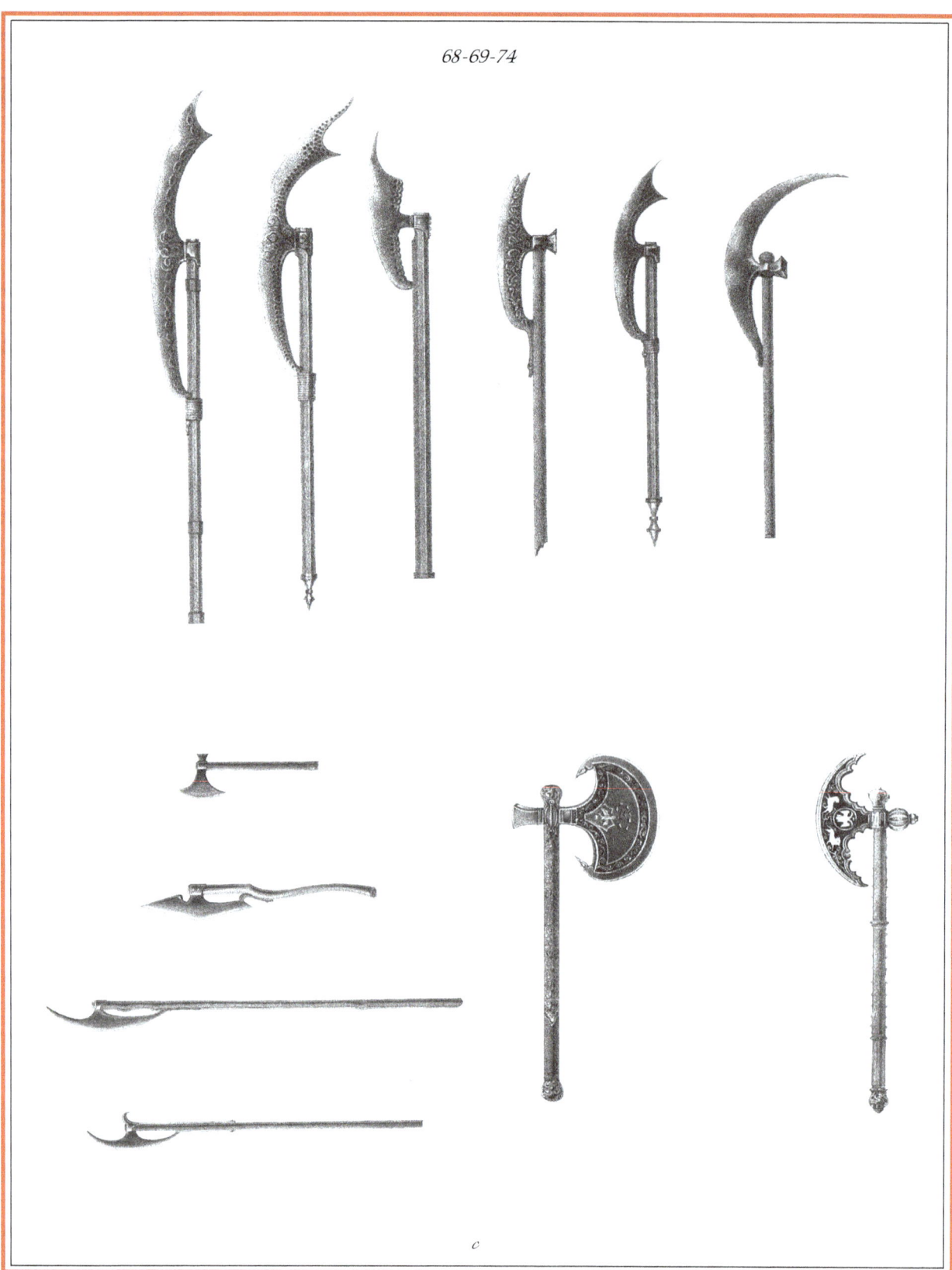

c

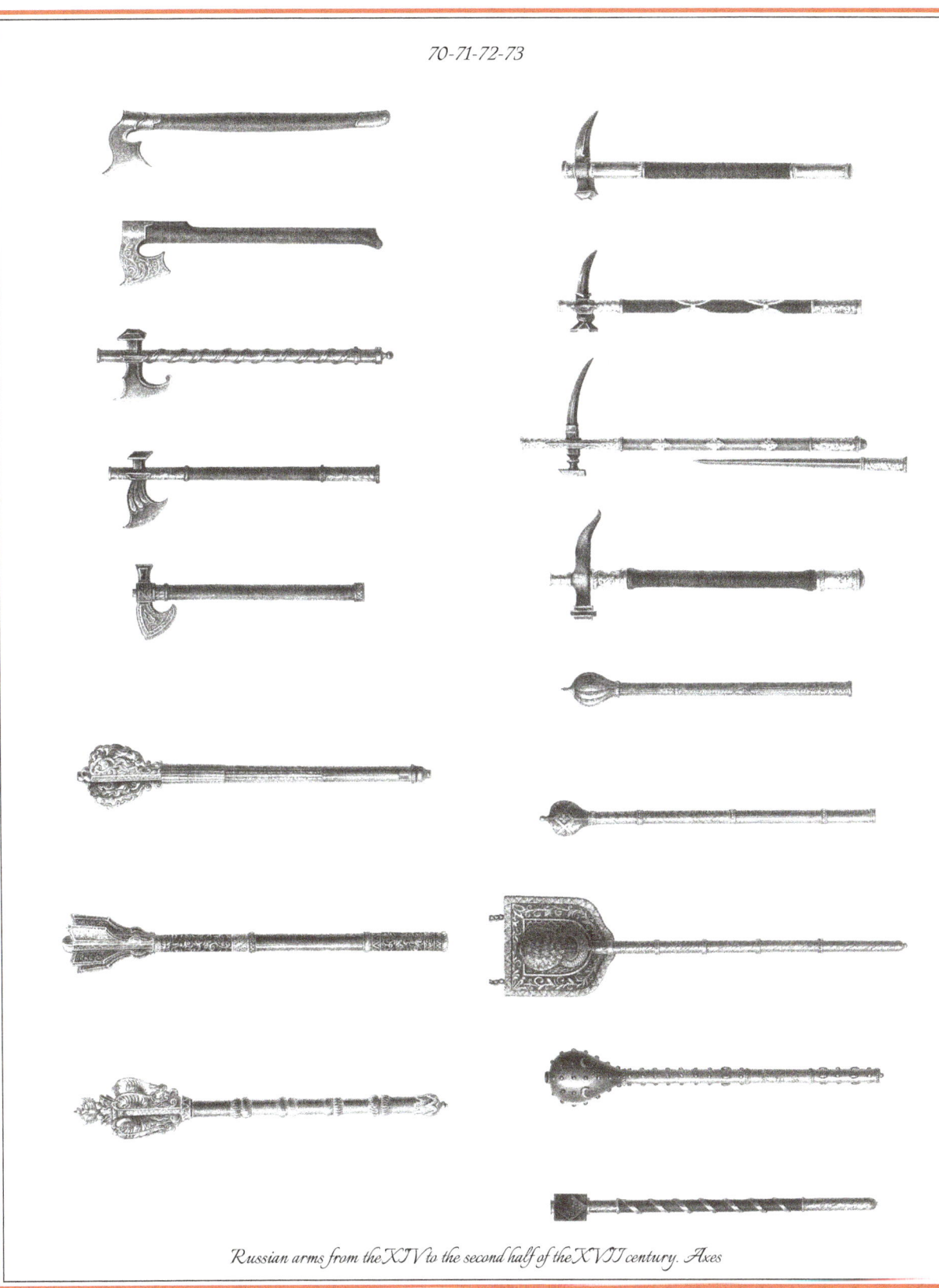

Russian arms from the XIV to the second half of the XVII century. Axes

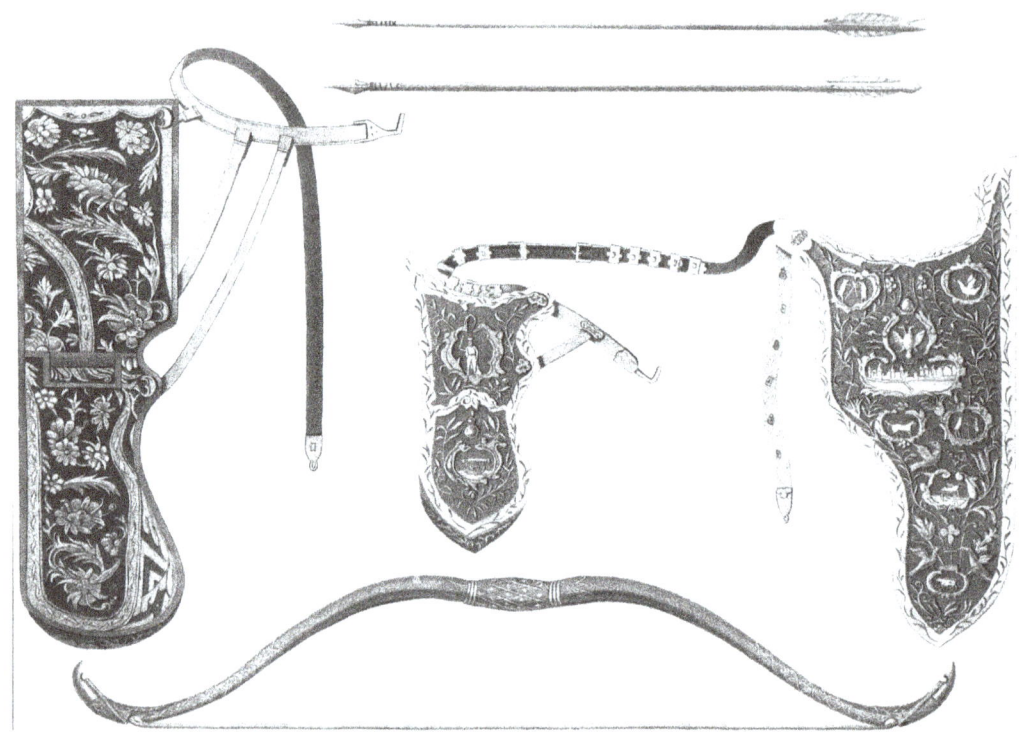

Russian arms from the XIV to the second half of the XVII century. Blow

TAccessories for weapons from the XIV to the second half of the XVII century. Pokrovets on Saadak.

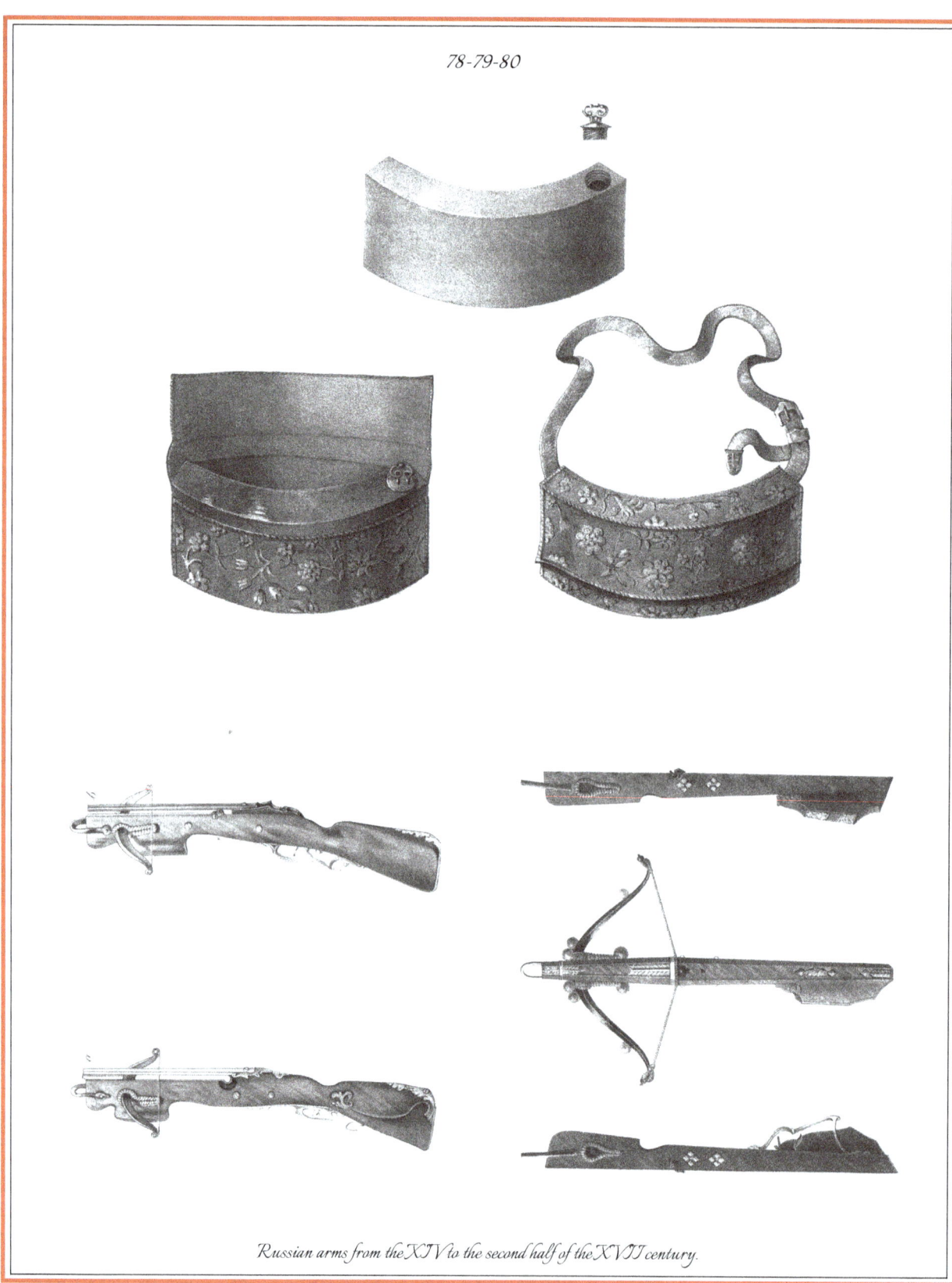

Russian arms from the XIV to the second half of the XVII century.

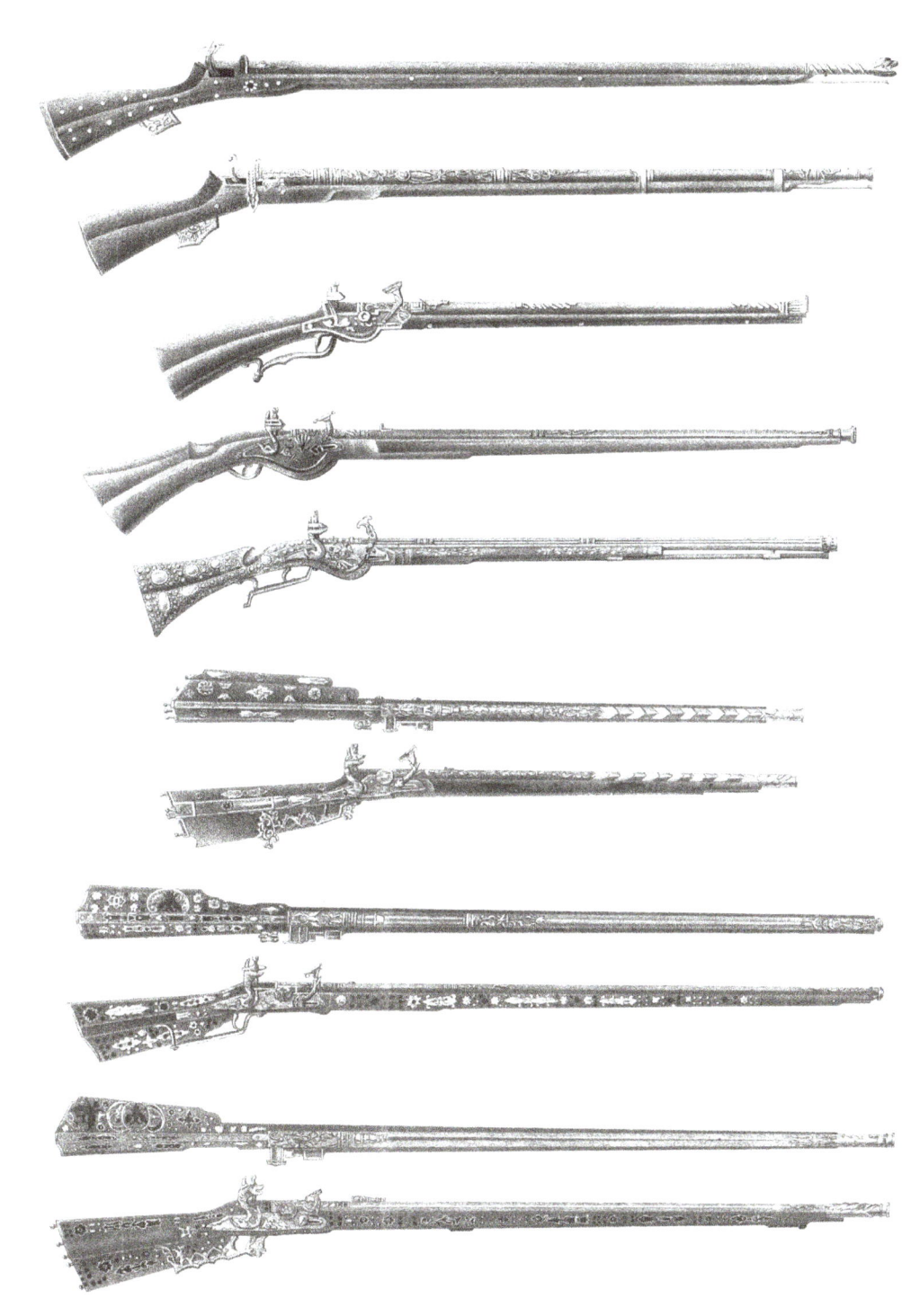

Russian firearms from the XIV to the second half of the XVII century.

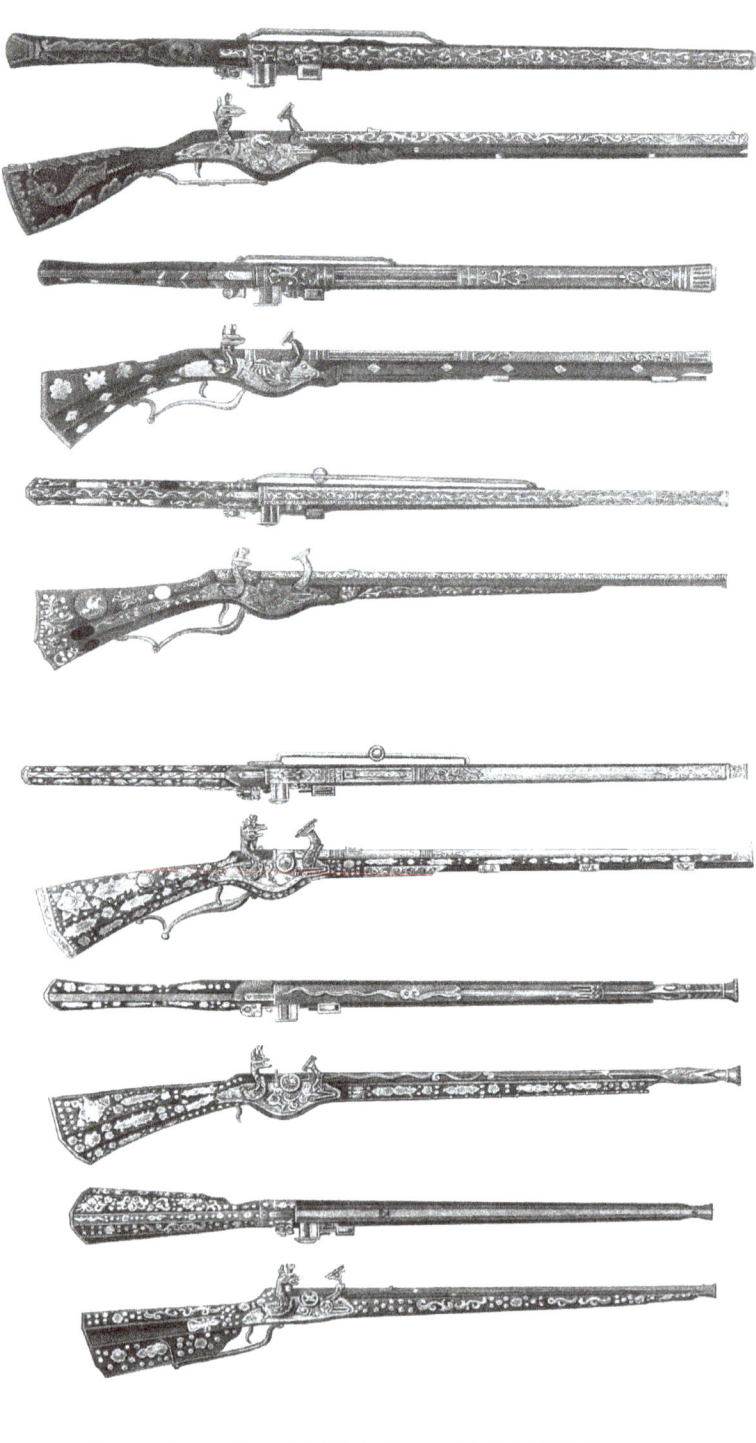

Russian firearms from the XIV to the second half of the XVII century.

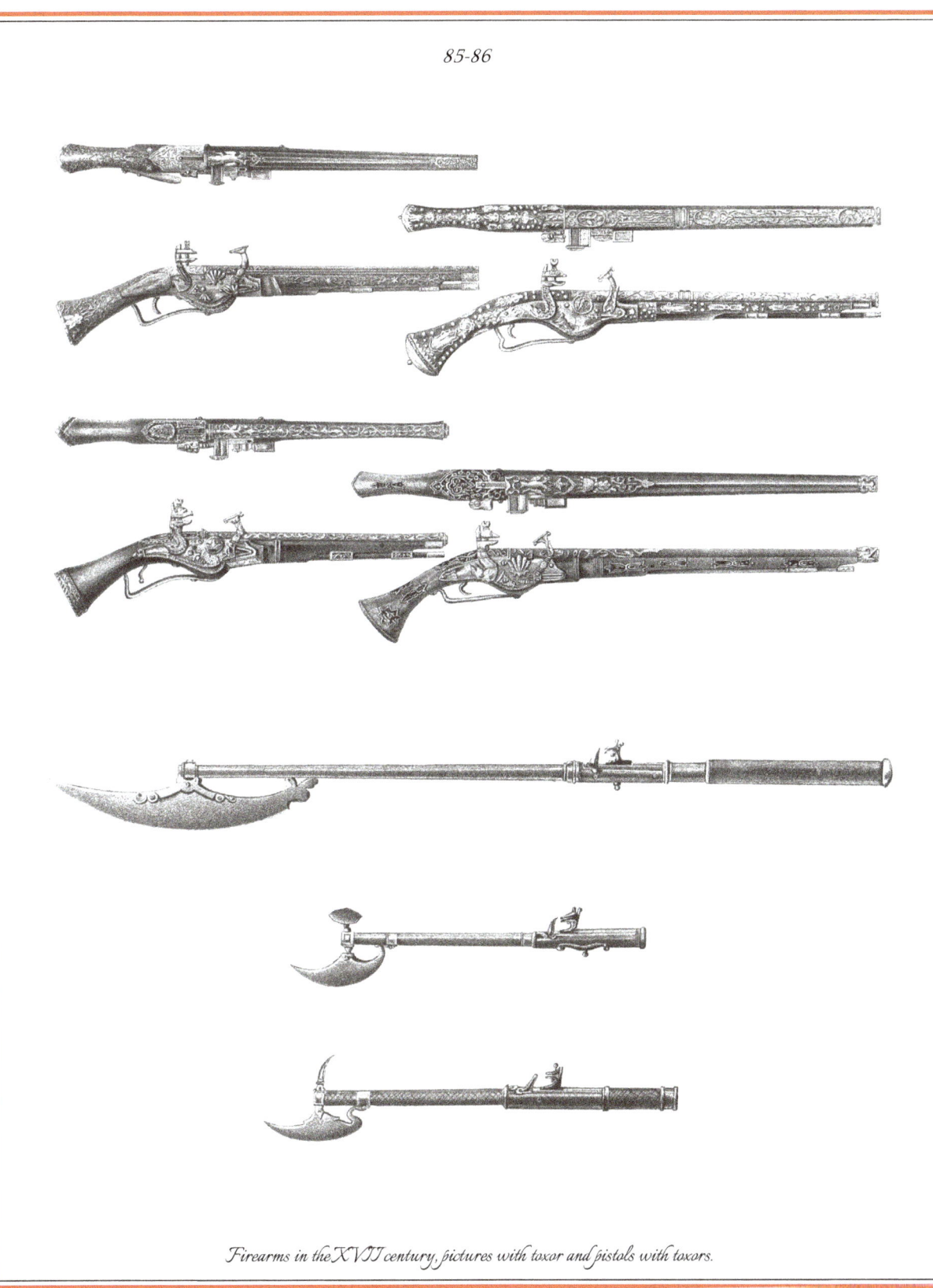

Firearms in the XVII century, pictures with toxor and pistols with toxors.

Accessories for firearms in the XV, XVI and XVII centuries, the Berendeyki.

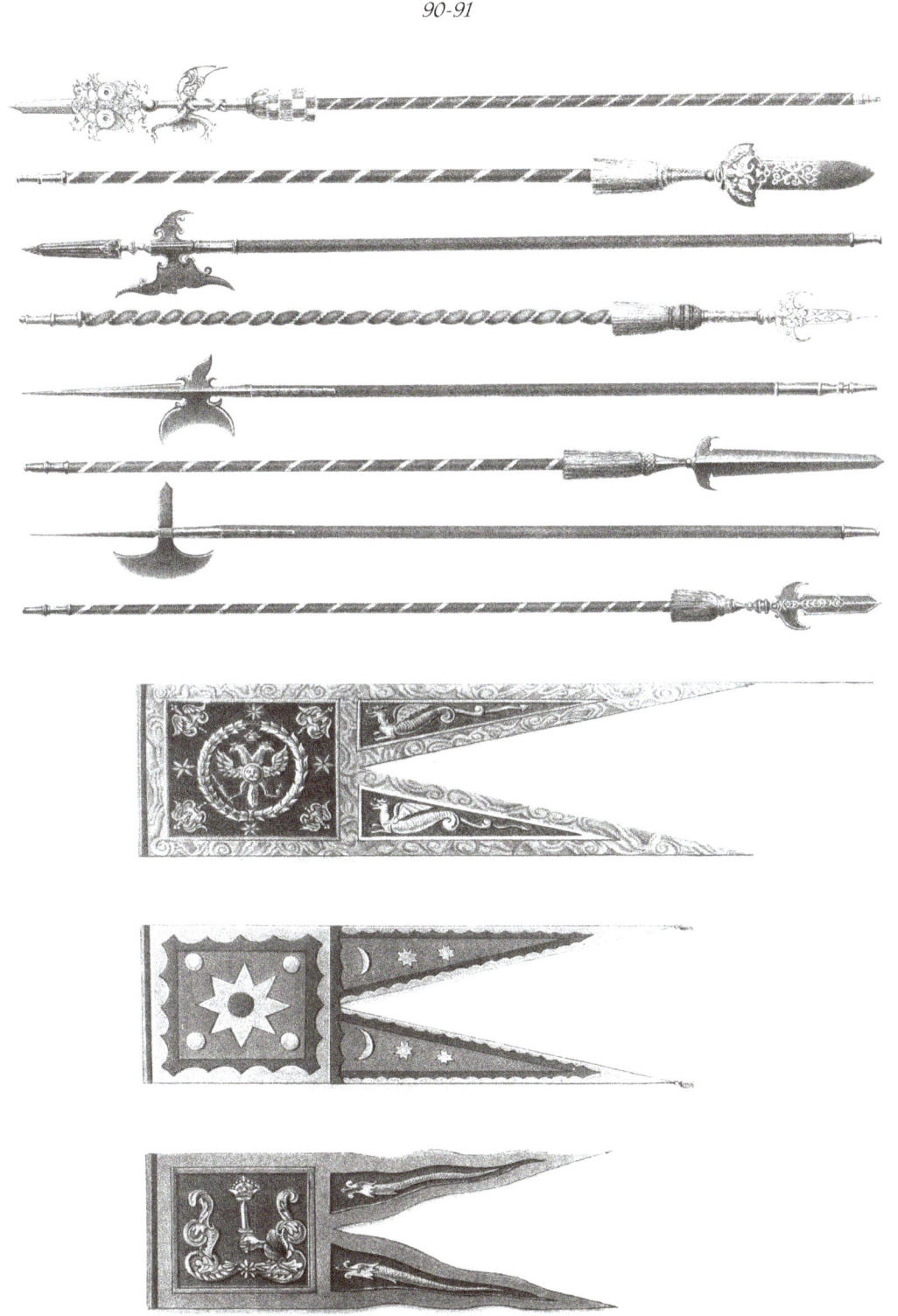

Russian armament of the XVII century. alebards and partizans. and flags

Russian arms from the XIV to the second half of the XVII century. the principles in the tegilies and the shapes of the irons.

Russian arms from the XIV to the second half of the XVII century. the prince in bakhters and in shishak with elite

Russian arms from the XIV to the second half of the XVII century. the battery and the shelm.

Russian arms from the XIV to the second half of the XVII century. the case with the barmitz and the paper shape.

Russian arms from the XIV to the second half of the XVII century

Russian arms from the XIV to the second half of the XVII century. Warrior in Yushman and in Misyurka.

Russian arms from the XIV to the second half of the XVII century. the harmony in the kuyak and the hair of the copper.

XIV to the XVII century. The Warrior in the Mirror and in the Sleeve. The view depicts part of the Moscow Kremlin in the XVII c.

Russian arms from the XIV to the second half of the XVII century. voevoda in two pancreas and in erihonk.

Russian arms from the XIV to the second half of the XVII century. voevoda in the mirror in the wire and in the erihonk.

Boyarin in the XVI and XVII centuries. (The view depicts part of the Kremlin from the side of Moskvorechye).

Rynda in the XVI and XVII centuries

Russian Guard in 1674

Russian horsemen in 1678

Streltsy in 1613. (The view depicts the Church of St. Basil the Blessed and the Kremlin wall in Moscow, at the beginning of the 17th century).

Guard in 1613 (The view depicts the courtyard before the former embassy home in Moscow).

Streltsy of the Moscow Strelets' Regiments Lutokhin and Ivan Poltev: in 1674.

Streltsy S of the Moscow Streletsky Regiments: Kolobov, Aleksandrov, Golovlinsky and Bukhvostov; In 1674.

Strelsy of the Moscow Strelets Regiments: Lagowskin, Vorontsov and Naramansky; In 1674.

Streltsy of the Moscow Strelets Regiments: Lagowskin, Vorontsov and Naramansky; In 1674.

Standarbearer and Streltsy of the moscow streetsky Levshin regiment, in 1674.

Initial people or officers of the Moscow Streletsky Regiments: in 1674.

German musketeer of a regiments, who were in the Russian service in the XVII century

German pikeman of a regiments, who were in the Russian service in the XVII century

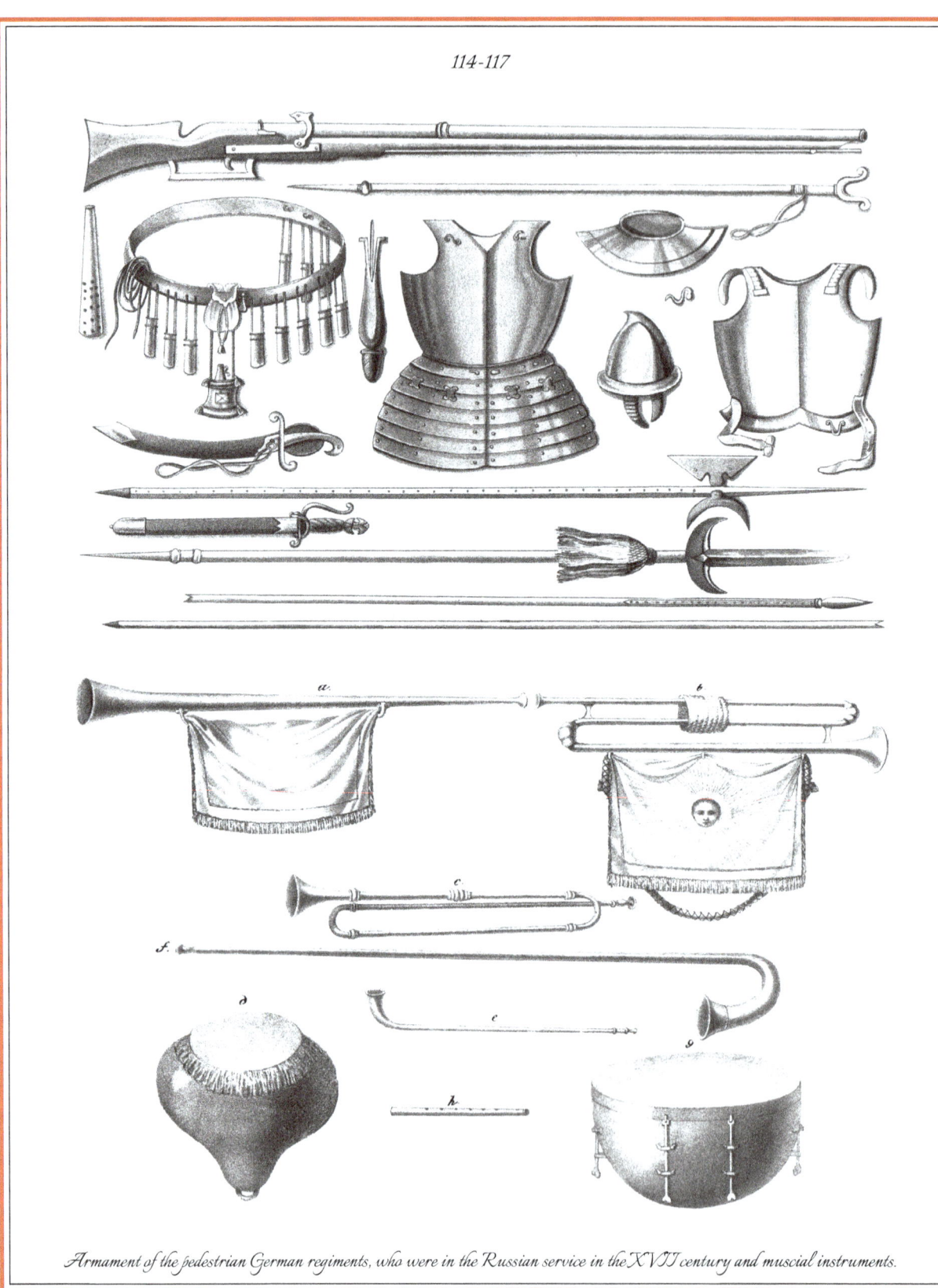

Armament of the pedestrian German regiments, who were in the Russian service in the XVII century and muscial instruments.

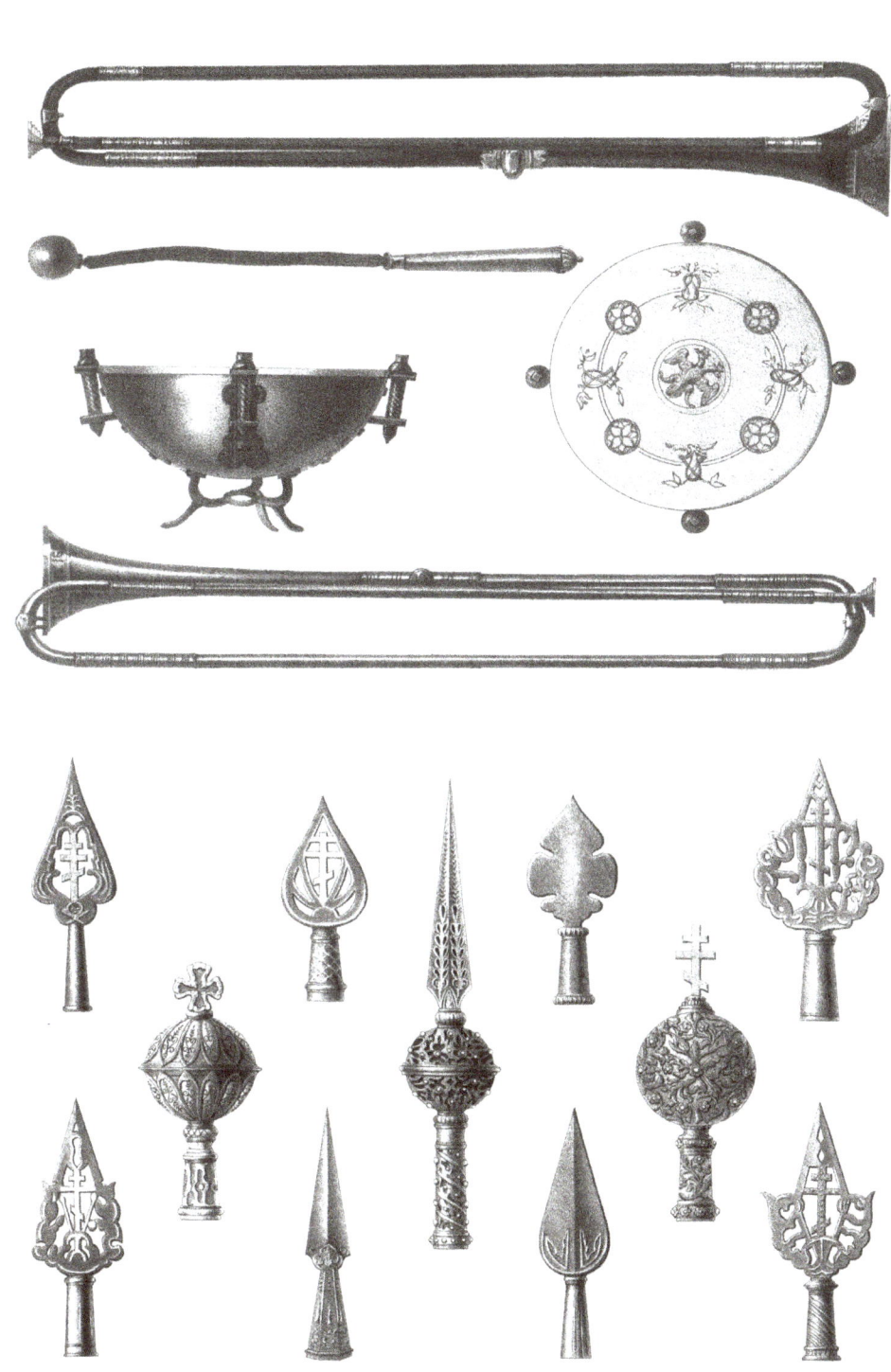

Musical instruments, used before the XVIII century in the armies and standard points

The banner of Prince Pozharsky, 1612.

Banner of the Tsar Joann Vasilyevich Grozny, 1560. - The Banner of Time of Tsar Alexei Mikhailovich, 1645-1676.

Banner of 1645-1676 years. and banner 1690

The banner of the reign of Tsar Peter Alekseevich, 1696-1699. - Banner of the Moscow Streltsy, 1699th year.

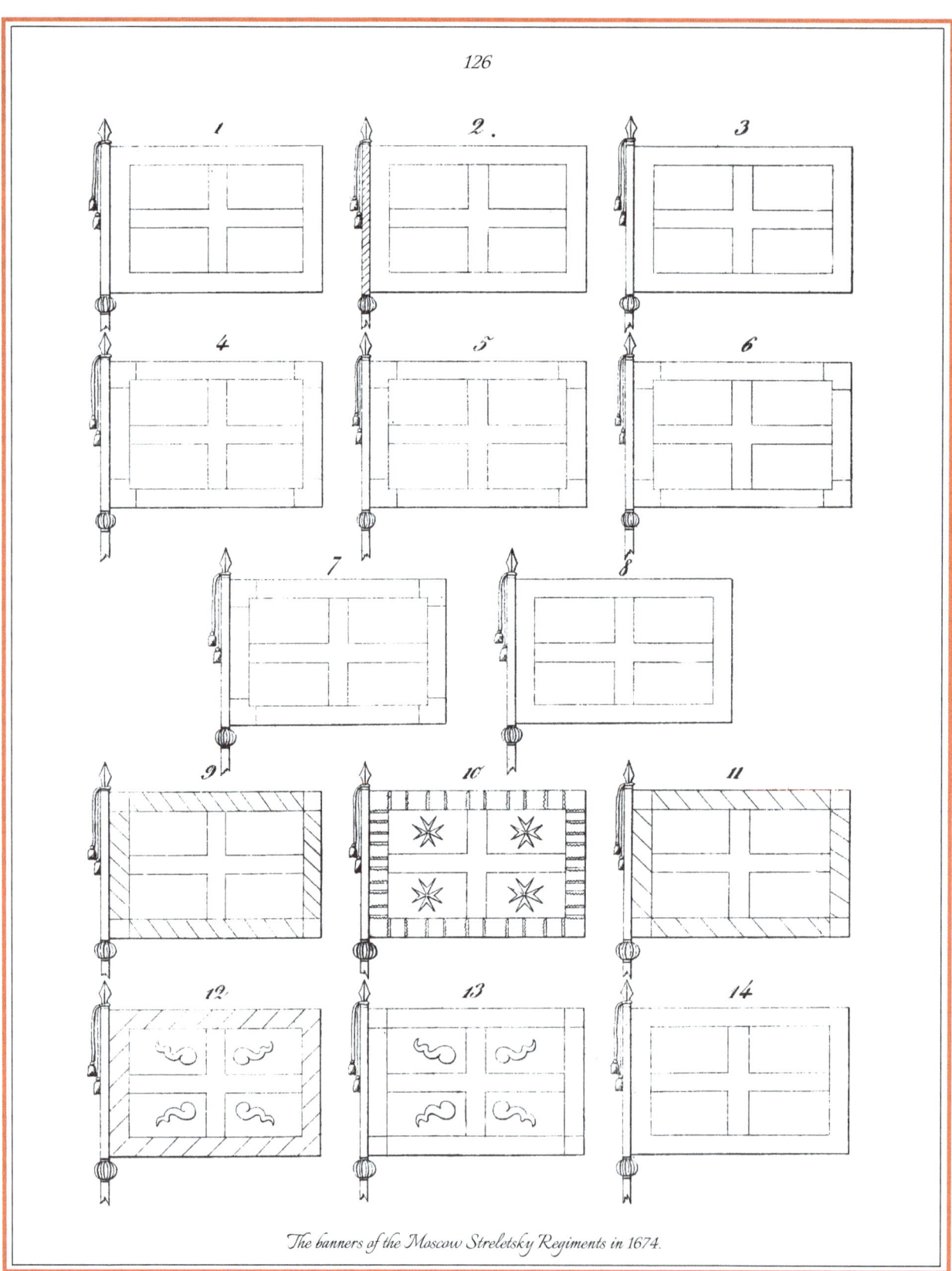

The banners of the Moscow Streletsky Regiments in 1674.

Banner of the Astrakhan Streltsy, 1693-th year.

The Banner of 1696. - Prapor XVII century.

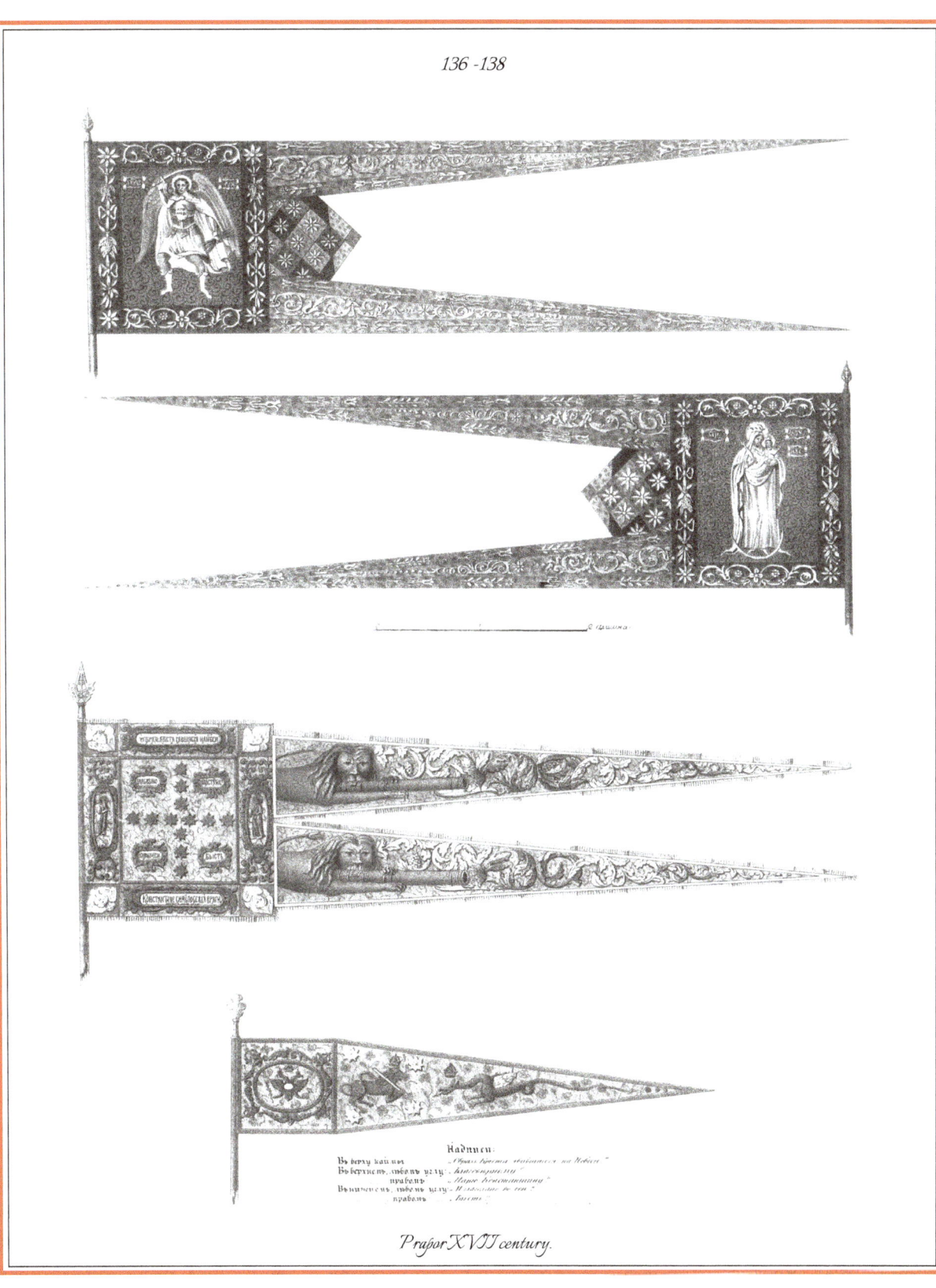

Prapor XVII century.

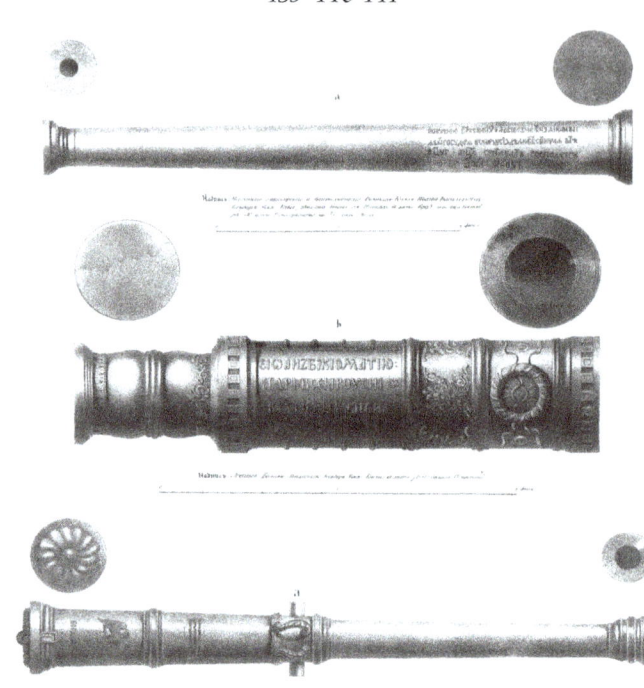

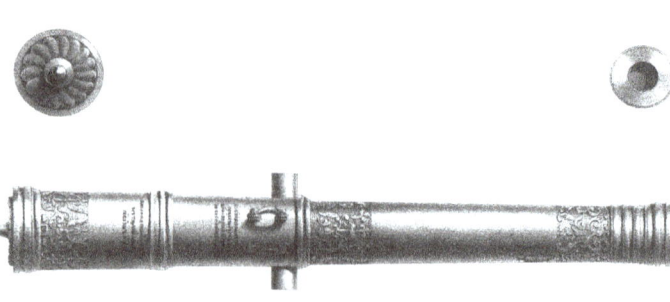

Various Russian guns and artillery from 1510 to 1695

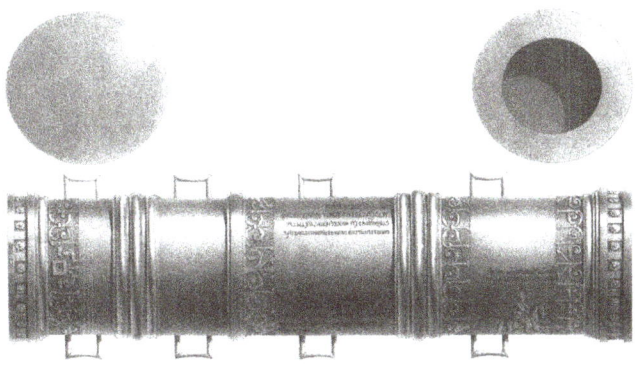

Надпись на разныхъ части: [illegible inscription text]

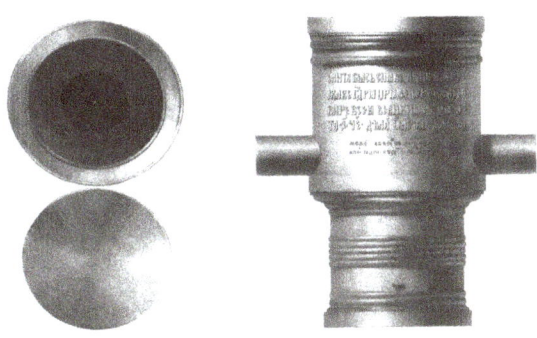

Надпись [illegible inscription text]

a

Надпись на верхней части: [illegible inscription text]

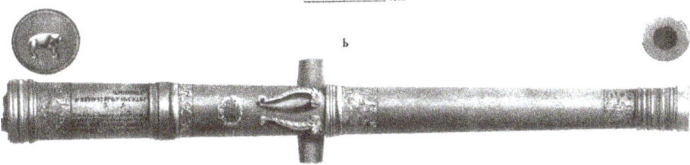

b

Надпись на нижней части: [illegible inscription text]

Various Russian guns and artillery from 1510 to 1695

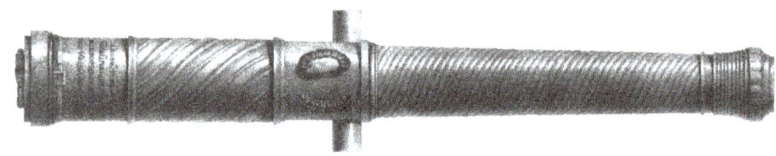

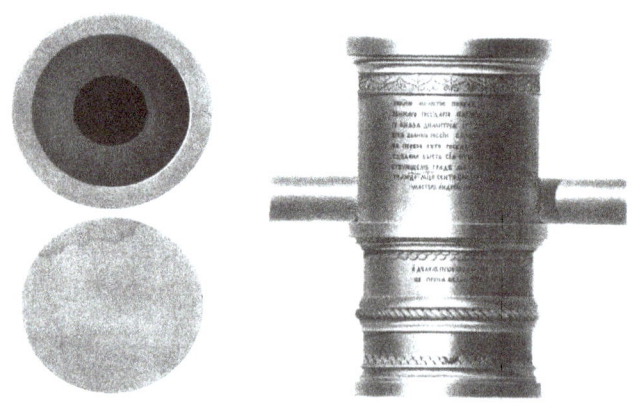

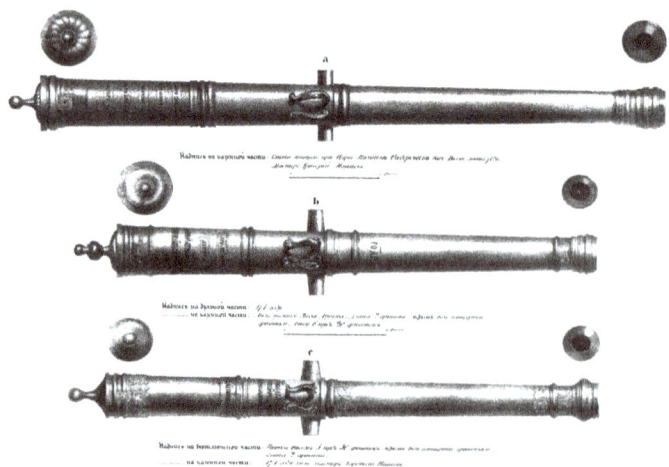

Various Russian guns and artillery from 1510 to 1695

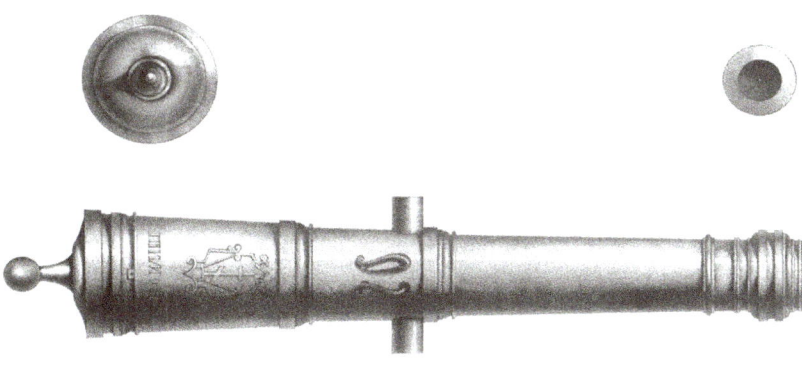

Various Russian guns and artillery from 1510 to 1695

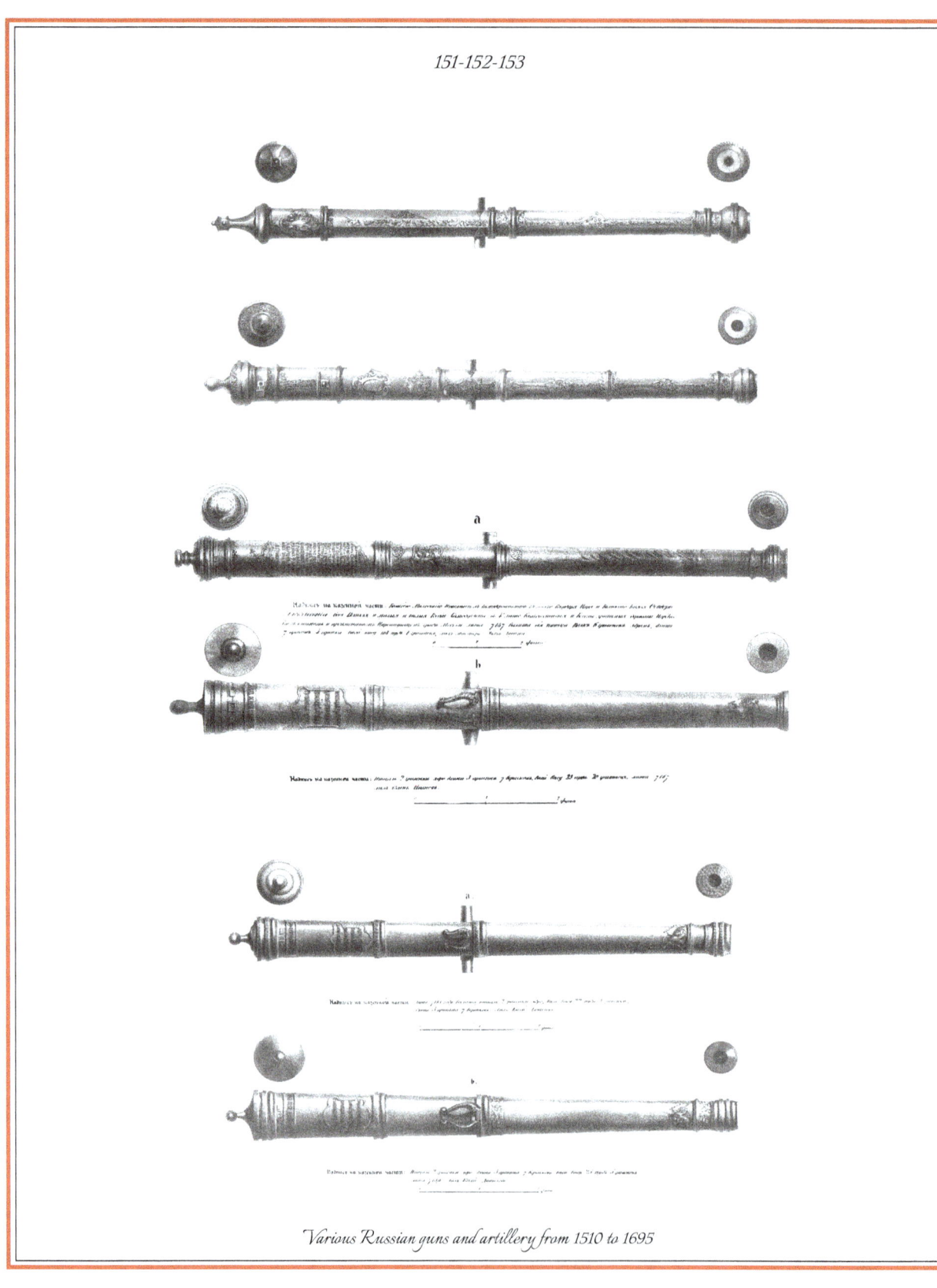

Various Russian guns and artillery from 1510 to 1695

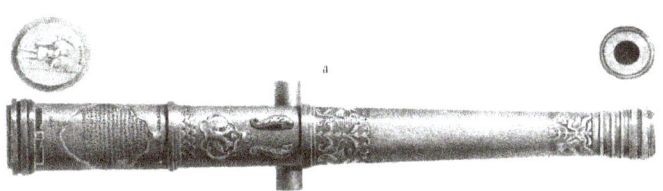

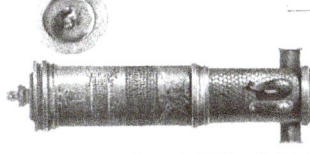

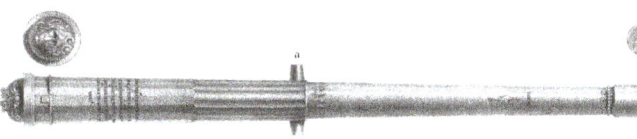

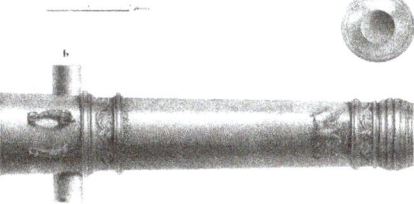

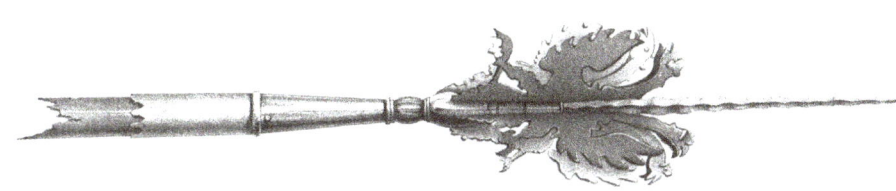

Various Russian guns and artillery from 1510 to 1695

SOLDIERS, WEAPONS & UNIFORMS ALREADY PUBLISHED
(SOME TITLES)

UNIFORMS OF RUSSIAN ARMY IN THE ERA OF ANCIENT TZAR
FROM THE REIGN OF VASILI IV TO MICHAEL I, ALEXIS, FEODOR III DURING THE XVII th CENTURY
A.V.VISKOVATOV   LUCA STEFANO CRISTINI
SWU-600-004

UNIFORMS OF RUSSIAN ARMY OF PETER I THE GREAT
FROM THE REIGN OF PETER I TO CATHERINE I, PEER II, ANNA AND IVAN VI, 1682-1741
A.V.VISKOVATOV   LUCA STEFANO CRISTINI
SWU-700-006

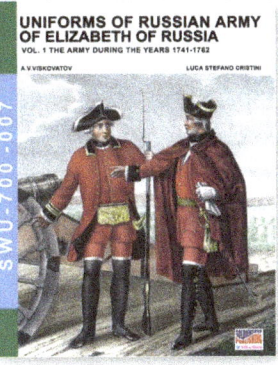

UNIFORMS OF RUSSIAN ARMY OF ELIZABETH OF RUSSIA
VOL.1 THE ARMY DURING THE YEARS 1741-1762
A.V.VISKOVATOV   LUCA STEFANO CRISTINI
SWU-700-007

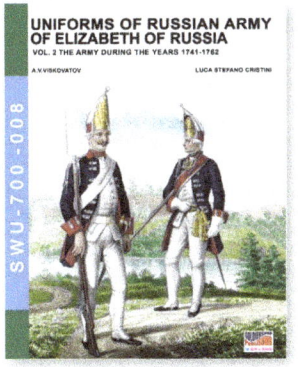

UNIFORMS OF RUSSIAN ARMY OF ELIZABETH OF RUSSIA
VOL.2 THE ARMY DURING THE YEARS 1741-1762
A.V.VISKOVATOV   LUCA STEFANO CRISTINI
SWU-700-008

UNIFORMS OF RUSSIAN ARMY IN THE XVIII CENTURY VOL.1
UNDER THE REIGN OF CATHERINE II EMPRESS OF RUSSIA BETWEEN 1762 AND 1796
A.V.VISKOVATOV - LUCA STEFANO CRISTINI
SWU-700-005

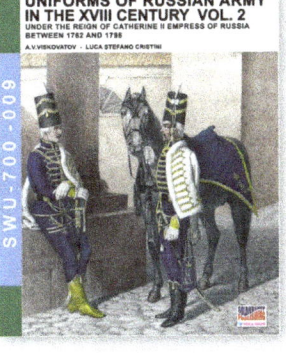

UNIFORMS OF RUSSIAN ARMY IN THE XVIII CENTURY VOL.2
UNDER THE REIGN OF CATHERINE II EMPRESS OF RUSSIA BETWEEN 1762 AND 1796
A.V.VISKOVATOV - LUCA STEFANO CRISTINI
SWU-700-009

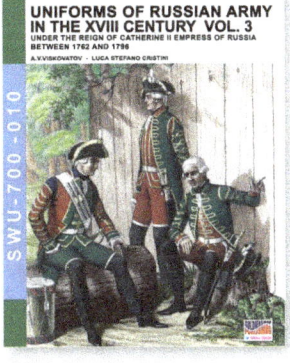

UNIFORMS OF RUSSIAN ARMY IN THE XVIII CENTURY VOL.3
UNDER THE REIGN OF CATHERINE II EMPRESS OF RUSSIA BETWEEN 1762 AND 1796
A.V.VISKOVATOV - LUCA STEFANO CRISTINI
SWU-700-010

UNIFORMS OF RUSSIAN ARMY IN THE XVIII CENTURY VOL.4
UNDER THE REIGN OF CATHERINE II EMPRESS OF RUSSIA BETWEEN 1762 AND 1796
A.V.VISKOVATOV - LUCA STEFANO CRISTINI
SWU-700-011

BRITISH ARMY UNIFORMS IN 1742
IN THE ART OF JOHN PINE
SWU-700-001

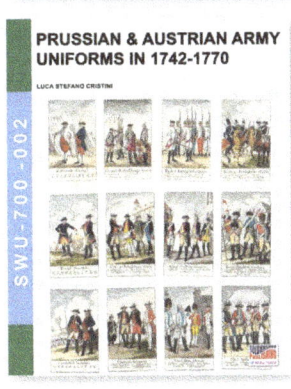

PRUSSIAN & AUSTRIAN ARMY UNIFORMS IN 1742-1770
LUCA STEFANO CRISTINI
SWU-700-002

THE FRENCH ARMY OF ANCIEN RÉGIME Volume 1
IN THE ART OF FELIX PHILIPPOTEAUX
LUCA STEFANO CRISTINI
SWU-700-003

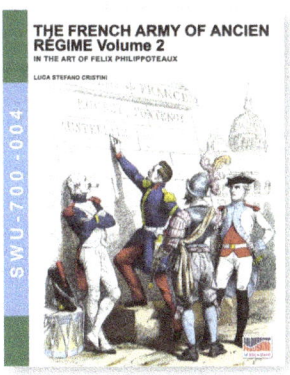

THE FRENCH ARMY OF ANCIEN RÉGIME Volume 2
IN THE ART OF FELIX PHILIPPOTEAUX
LUCA STEFANO CRISTINI
SWU-700-004

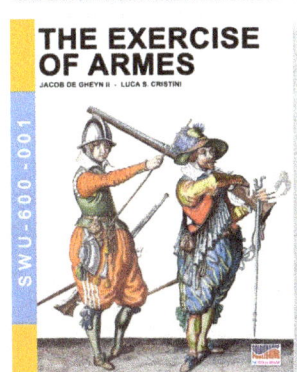

THE EXERCISE OF ARMES
JACOB DE GHEYN II - LUCA S. CRISTINI
SWU-600-001

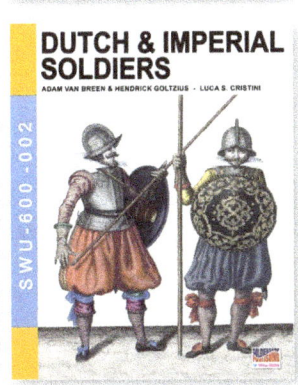

DUTCH & IMPERIAL SOLDIERS
ADAM VAN BREEN & HENDRICK GOLTZIUS - LUCA S. CRISTINI
SWU-600-002

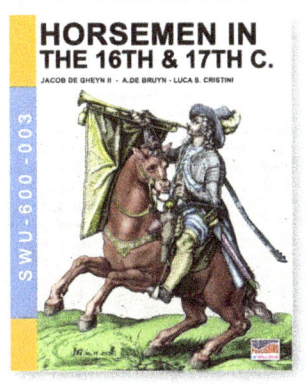

HORSEMEN IN THE 16TH & 17TH C.
JACOB DE GHEYN II - A.DE BRUYN - LUCA S. CRISTINI
SWU-600-003

IMPERIAL SOLDIERS & UNIFORMS 1640-1860
IN THE ART OF FRANZ GERASCH
LUCA S. CRISTINI   Plates by FRANZ GERASCH
SWU-GEN-001